This is a story of hope: a story of life as journey, where nothing has the final reminds us how unimagined changes await us just beyond our view if we will only continue daring. Writing with frank honesty, she lifts the lid on what goes on behind so many closed doors, giving us important insight into the power the past can wield over our present, irrespective of faith and theology. In reality, being a Christian can only ever involve being fully human while adoring the divine. Greta's humble openness will empower the one in four women and one in eight men who have suffered their own sexual abuses by letting them know they are not in isolation, while also providing life-giving insights to those who walk knowingly and unknowingly alongside the many sufferers of this major human rights epidemic that is a poisonous axle of our cultural psyche. You will grow as you read.
Maggie Ellis, Director, Lifecentre Rape Crisis, psychosexual therapist, agony aunt for Christianity *magazine*

Greta has suffered the devastating effects of ongoing abuse and subsequently the misery of long-term depression. Her story is told vividly and honestly, not seeking to hide the pain of her experience, but aiming to redeem it in the hope of bringing healing and freedom to others. It is an authentic story that will clearly resonate with many people, and one that will affect many more. This is a powerful and moving personal tale of the amazing freedom and life that forgiveness can bring in the name of Jesus Christ.
Ali Herbert, freelance writer and author of Worth Knowing: Wisdom for Women

This book provides a moving and at times disturbing insight into the life of a victim of sexual abuse. After years of merely surviving, amidst confusion, depression and anger, Greta discovered forgiveness as a major turning point in her walk of

personal freedom. Forgiveness did and does not mean denying the need for justice – nor is it something easily achieved in the face of such suffering – yet Greta's story is a powerful reminder that the walk of freedom and fullness of life in Christ are found, at least in part, through the difficult duty of forgiveness.
Hanni Seddon, School of Ministry Pastor, St Aldates Church, Oxford

I can think of several people who will really be helped in their journey by this book. Those suffering the pain of sexual abuse, and their husbands and wives, will find not only understanding in this most courageous and honest book, but also sexual hope: a rainbow of hope from God that arcs from its pages towards the reader out of the crucible of the author's former darkness.
Dr Trevor Stammers, Senior Tutor in General Practice, St George's, University of London and Lecturer in Healthcare Ethics, St Mary's University College

Royalties

All royalties from the sale of this book go to The Helping Hands Project in Andhra Pradesh, India, a self-sufficiency venture, teaching widows to sew, and enabling the purchase of sewing machines.

Greta Randle

Forgiving the Impossible?

From abuse
to
freedom & hope

ivp

INTER-VARSITY PRESS
Norton Street, Nottingham NG7 3HR, England
Email: ivp@ivpbooks.com
Website: www.ivpbooks.com

The names of key non-family members have been deliberately altered to protect
the identities of those concerned.

British Library Cataloguing in Publication Data
A catalogue record for this book is available from the British Library.

ISBN: 978-1-84474-433-6

Set in 11.5/14pt Chaparral
Typeset by CRB Associates, Potterhanworth, Lincolnshire
Printed by Ashford Colour Press Ltd, Gosport, Hampshire

*Inter-Varsity Press publishes Christian books that are true to the Bible and that
communicate the gospel, develop discipleship and strengthen the church for its
mission in the world.*

*Inter-Varsity Press is closely linked with the Universities and Colleges Christian
Fellowship, a student movement connecting Christian Unions in universities and
colleges throughout Great Britain, and a member movement of the International
Fellowship of Evangelical Students. Website: www.uccf.org.uk*

Contents

Acknowledgments

Ian and I have now been married for thirty-nine years. He has stuck by me through everything, despite the roughest of times between 1985 and 1990 and from 1994 to 2003. I am deeply grateful for the relationship that we now enjoy. Thank you, Ian, for being willing for us to work things out together.

Our sons continue to be a great delight to me, and now I have the added joy of their wives and children in my life too. Adam, Timothy and Nathan, you have your own feelings and experiences of how it was in the family home. I trust that our mutual relationships have offset some of the potential damage of what happened to me as it was played out in front of you all.

The seedling thought of writing a book grew as I became more and more whole. It was confirmed to me about four years ago when one of the leaders in our church said, 'A book will come out of this, Greta.' Thank you, Lee, for hearing the prompting of the Holy Spirit and for sharing it with me.

There are two people who have become household names in our family: 'Rosie the reader' and 'Eleanor the editor'. Rosie is a new friend whom God brought into my life through work. She has been such an encourager. As each chapter has been written, she has read it through and made helpful comments. Thank you, Rosie, for giving your help even when times were tough for you. Eleanor is also a new friend. We met at a day conference and began talking about the possibility of writing. She has been at the end of a phone or email whenever I have wanted to talk things through. She has given me helpful advice and made suggestions, and has kept her professional eye on me. Thank you, Eleanor, for sharing your nuggets of wisdom and helping me to focus on the elements that make a good book.

An old friend too has been involved in the final preparations. Sue and I have known each other since about 1982. We were both young mums then and supported each other at various times. Sue teaches English and has helped enormously by paying meticulous attention to my punctuation and grammar and giving me tips on creative writing.

I have also needed practical help at times. The one task that slipped while I was writing was the ironing. My sister has taken several piles and returned everything beautifully pressed and ready to wear. Thank you, Zillah, for your help, which gave me the extra time I needed.

Technological support has come from Paul, a colleague. He has taught me about merging documents, contents pages and headings. Thank you so much, Paul, for 'playing' with each of these pages, but the bad news is that I can't remember it all and will need you for the next book too!

Thank you to so many people who have enquired about the progress of the book, showing interest without interference.

Special thanks go to my brother and each of my sisters. You had no reservations about this book and actively encouraged me to go ahead. You have trusted me. However, what follows is my perspective, and you may well have different feelings about our home and family and the things about which I have written. Thank you all. I hope that your faith in me has not been misplaced and that you will find that the book holds something for you too.

Above all else, I want to thank God. My healing would have been only partial without divine intervention. Self-help, counselling and reading have all played a part, but nothing can take the place that God occupied within the whole process. He spoke to me through his word; he used his people to pray with me; he was constant. Some may raise the question, 'Why does God allow these things?' It is my perception that it hurts God to know that the people he created allow themselves to do 'these things'. It was never his wish for me to be damaged as a child, but he is a sovereign God and able to redeem every situation, however sinful.

> . . . find the way
> to healthy
> wholeness
> and having found it,
> take others with you,
> get out of the box
> then go back in
> and get
> your
> brother.
> (written by Ruth Reeve)

Greta Randle
January 2010

The author can be contacted on:
greta.randle@ntlworld.com

Foreword

This is no ordinary book. Neither is it a book for everyone. Moreover, it is not an easy read. It is graphic and detailed. You may not be prepared for what follows. I say this because not all of us have suffered in the manner described. This book is directed towards those who have gone through such pain as the author describes. Those who have been abused as she was will take comfort from reading it.

We are living in an era when sexual abuse exists almost around every corner. It is found in middle-class families, even among 'Christian' people whom you would never suspect to be so tainted. Many have a story to tell – but keep quiet about it. Those who have been abused often blame themselves and hide the facts for years and years. Some never talk about it at all.

But author Greta Randle has decided to talk about it. She is Chief Executive of the Association of Christian Counsellors, a group that represents Christian counsellors and pastoral ministries. Greta is married to Ian, a church minister for some fifteen years. She was a social worker before taking up her present position, and has had particular experience as a senior practitioner working with disabled children.

Greta has decided to tell her story, a stunning if not shocking account of a life that has known suffering, beginning with sexual abuse. Writing a book like this has required great skill and sensitivity, relaying to the reader accounts of the most delicate situations.

It is also a story of forgiveness. This is where I come in and the reason no doubt why I have been asked to write this foreword. I have known nothing personally of sexual abuse. But I do know what it is to forgive, as I describe in my own book *Total Forgiveness*.[1] The greatest benefit of forgiveness comes not so much to the person who is forgiven but to the one who does the forgiving. It is what sets one free. A further reason for forgiveness, moreover, is to keep us from being outwitted by Satan (2 Corinthians 2:11), for the devil will seize upon any measure of unforgiveness in us.

Greta has had to do a lot of forgiving. The value of this book, therefore, lies not only in finding comfort from knowing someone who has been abused, perhaps as you have been, but in coming through this by forgiving those who have been so horrible. I have taught for years that the greater the suffering, the greater the anointing. If you have suffered, and dignified the trial, there is blessing for you. The blessing could be greater than you ever dreamed. All things work together for good for those who love God and who are called according to his purpose (Romans 8:28).

I pray that this book will give you hope and comfort, but also that you will be led to forgive those who have hurt you. You will be the blessed one in this case, and can even thank God that suffering is not for nothing, but that it can be used to bring comfort to others: 'For just as the sufferings of Christ flow over into our lives, so also through Christ our comfort overflows' (2 Corinthians 1:5).

R. T. Kendall
Minister and author

Preface

This book, with its obvious limitations, cannot adequately describe the ghastly depths I reached during the years of depression. However, the same is also true of the elation I often feel at being free from it! The limitations also mean that there are many, many more things that happened and conversations that took place which are too numerous to mention. But I trust that what follows will convey the essential elements to the reader.

'Depression' is a term that is maligned, misused and mis-understood. It is not an 'off' day, nor is it something that can easily be shrugged off, and there is no way that sufferers can 'pull themselves together' or just 'get over it'. Depression is a strong and powerful force. It wraps itself around the body and mind with a vice-like grip. It is dark and foreboding.

Behind the Smile was the title I originally suggested for this book because that has been the story of my life: just smile to cover the hurt; smile and no-one will guess there is pain; just smile and continue as normal. Just keep smiling and I might even be able to convince *myself* that all is well. I called myself 'the eternal optimist', but, ever persistent, it caught up even with me . . . Depression!

Eliciting sympathy is not the object of this book. Sharing my story springs from a deep desire to bring hope to others who may have experienced similar horrors. In the New Testament, Paul speaks of God as 'the Father of compassion and the God of all comfort, who comforts us in all our troubles, so that we can comfort those in any trouble with the comfort we ourselves have received from God'. It is my heartfelt prayer that this book will bring real comfort and hope to fellow sufferers.[1] 'May the God of hope fill you with all joy and peace as you trust in him, so that you may overflow with hope . . . ' (Romans 15:13).

Introduction

I was crying. It took me by complete surprise and I was embarrassed. One minute I was talking and the next minute I couldn't say a word. Seated opposite the social worker, tears streaming down my face and sobs catching in my throat, I clutched a large, white, man-sized handkerchief and collected the drips from my nose.

The dog was lying on the floor. Normally the house was quiet only in school time but even then I often had the radio on or music playing. We were a busy, noisy household: three boys, a dog and a cat. Sometimes we had a student or another young person living with us. At other times we had families from our church round to share a meal, or the boys had schoolfriends for tea and to play. Then there was a variety of instruments being played at varying levels of competence: a drum kit, a clarinet, a violin and a piano.

But today was different. I had been asked a simple question, and when I had opened my mouth to speak I had fallen headlong into a huge chasm of emotion.

Over the years my husband, Ian, and I had talked about fostering children. We had followed this up by making a couple of phone calls to social services on two separate occasions. However our enquiries never seemed to reach the right department. No-one returned the calls and there was no further contact. It seemed that our willingness to explore the possibility of offering our home to other children was simply being ignored.

But this was 'third time lucky'. We had passed the first hurdle of an initial visit and our details had been passed to the local fostering and adoption team. Unknown to us at the time, we had to wait for our 'case' to be allocated to a social worker with a specific remit for doing assessments.

Our three sons were twelve, seven and four years old. We had talked with them about the idea, explaining why some parents were sometimes not able to look after their children. We spoke of what it would mean for us as a family to invite another child into our home. We talked about bedroom arrangements and sharing toys, and how they might want to identify some special things that were *not* to be shared. We spoke about social worker visits and parents seeing their children in our home. We tried to give them as much information as we could from our limited knowledge.

We had been briefed on the fostering application process. We would have several meetings with our social worker. Our family values would be assessed: our standard of parenting, the accommodation we could offer, and how we all inter-acted as a family. The people we had identified to act as referees for our good character would be interviewed. We would be required to attend a series of group sessions with two other social workers leading the discussions while also making their own assessment of us as a couple.

It was certainly clear that this was not an exercise for the faint-hearted. Long before we could even set eyes on a child in need of a home, we had to demonstrate commitment to a process that in itself would provide evidence that we had the necessary stamina for working with children.

And that wasn't all! The gathered information would become a report to be presented to a panel who would then make the final decision. It was a journey of many months that was already having a major emotional impact on me.

During this particular visit, Audrey, our social worker, had told us that we would be concentrating on our early years. We knew that we would have to speak individually about growing up, our parents, siblings and schools, and follow in any direction that the conversation took us. We were comfortable with Audrey. She was a good listener, jotting down notes, on occasion stopping to ask a question or to clarify something. She was analysing and probing but we knew it was all for a good cause. She had to know that we were the right kind of people. She had to make sure that we were not hiding anything.

It had started so well: 'Tell me about your childhood.' Simple! I told her about our family. I talked about my sisters and how we all related. I talked about our camaraderie but also our rivalry. When speaking of my younger brother, I added there had also been an older brother who had died before I was born.

I described school and my mediocre achievements there, recalling a time when, as a very young child, I was terrorised by a school bully.

I spoke of how my love of music had developed, those times of being alone in the front room of our family's terraced house playing the piano, and I gave her an insight into how I had discovered I was particularly gifted at 'playing by ear'.

There were happy times on picnics, with Dad pumping up the primus stove and Mum in charge of the Manchester tart, and games of cricket and the annual ritual of Dad buying each of us a season ticket for the local outdoor swimming baths.

I laughed as I described how my brother had dug up the small garden plots Dad had given each of us because he wanted to see if the plants were growing. I described the plethora of home-grown fruit and vegetables we enjoyed thanks to my dad.

Sad times featured too, especially the time when my kitten had to be put to sleep. I spoke of the extended family: my grandparents, who lived next door to us, and their Hillman car which Grandpa drove at an alarming speed. I told Audrey of the impact of my grandma's death and how I was desperate to see her even though I knew she had died, but that this was not a topic up for discussion with children in the 1950s. I described how my bachelor uncle, who lived with my grandparents, was often in our house and became almost like a third parent.

And then I tried to tell her that I had never had a birthday party. It felt important to admit it, although part of me thought it was disloyal to my parents. I felt almost compelled to get this skeleton out of its cupboard, to own and face it. A niggling voice was saying, 'You've been let down – all children have birthday parties, but not you.'

But why was I so distressed? After all, I was speaking of events from forty years ago! Why could I not speak of my birthdays? What had stirred such a strong reaction?

My spoken words were muffled and quiet and no-one spoke. My sobs and sniffs broke the silence and the un-answered questions hung in the air. What on earth was happening?

1 'It's a girl!'

It was Saturday lunchtime, time for the traditional working-class Saturday lunch of fish and chips. But on that day in May 1952 fish and chips were probably the last things on the minds of the family that lived at number 69. The house was buzzing, a midwife was in attendance (ironically called Nurse Borne), and saucepans of hot water were being boiled – the usual procedure on such occasions.

The three older girls were eight, four, and two. None was fully aware of what was going on and, unknown to them, their number had been added to with the birth of another girl. I arrived healthy and weighing in at a bouncy ten pounds. I was a wanted child, deliberately conceived, for, after all, I might have been a boy!

A few years earlier the family had looked quite different. Roger was the eldest, Sheila next and then Zillah, the youngest. Roger had developed an illness which had affected his heart. He was off school for a long time and had to be nursed over many months. Sadly he died at the age of only eight and half.

It is difficult to gauge the full impact of Roger's death on the family. He was remembered and spoken of, and very occasionally as children we would be privy to seeing his first baby shoes or his school books. There were letters of condolence and cards from his schoolfriends, carefully kept over the years in the sideboard. However, despite a certain amount of openness on the part of my mother, Dad never spoke of his first son.

After Roger's death there was a series of babies. Dad so wanted a boy but there were two more girls: Margaret and then me. Finally, there was a boy, following whom there were no more children. After all, there was no need. Adrian was the apple of Dad's eye.

Antenatal care, childbirth and the post-natal period were very different in the 1950s. Mums were prescribed a great deal of bed rest after the birth and fed a light diet of gruel. Customs surrounded the birth, such as 'being churched', which involved a visit to a church when the mother left the nursing home or hospital. A minister would pray over the mother and her new arrival in a ceremony of cleansing before they went back into their own home. And then there was 'shortening'. Both girls and boys were dressed in gowns or dresses as babies. When the mother saw fit she would begin to dress a boy in rompers and other clothes that denoted his gender. Some boys were two or even older before they were 'shortened'.

Following my birth I was introduced to my older sisters. Zillah walked into the room where Mum was being nursed during the post-natal 'lying-in' period. Mum called her over to the bed: 'Come and see what I've got.' She lifted the bedclothes and there I was, all snuggled and warm.

Our house was of an old style: front room, middle room and kitchen, one behind the other. There were three bedrooms upstairs: one at the front of the house and then a long landing leading to the other two. We had no bathroom.

Outside there was a paved area which we called 'the yard', leading to a coal house, a toilet and a wooden shed with an aviary attached. The aviary looked out onto a square lawn surrounded by flower beds. The largest of the beds led onto a large area of garden which was populated by several apple trees. Two of these remained for the whole time my mother lived in that house but the others were chopped down, for reasons unknown to me. Between the trees there was a variety of vegetables. Then there was a patch separated by a small fence, which Dad had dug over to give each of us a small area of garden.

Starting school was a milestone. The day I started, my older sisters had chicken pox and were not able to attend. Mum and I walked down the road and over the canal bridge and into the playground. As we walked into the building I was struck by the large number of children in the room. The tables were low and square, with small chairs set around them and an equally small child on each chair. It was a hive of activity and colour. I can only assume that I was late arriving because of my mother's dilemma about what to do about caring for my sisters. I was blissfully unaware that I would be left at school for the day. However I knew something was afoot. When I realised that my mother had left the room I became quite distressed. But Mrs McNally had seen it all before and was able to settle me in and occupy me with a set of large wooden beads.

In my second year I spent several weeks off school as all the children in our family came into contact with a skin parasite known as scabies. Besides being intensely irritating and itchy, it was also highly contagious.

While off school we developed a routine. During school time we were allowed to play outside. When school time was over and children spilled out onto the streets, we were confined to our own garden and home. Some days Mum would take us on long walks, pushing the large coach-built pram in which our young brother sat, with us tripping alongside, running on ahead or lagging behind. The infection didn't seem to have any impact on our energy levels.

Every day our bed sheets had to be ironed and sprinkled with DDT powder. Each evening Mum bathed us and, taking a huge jar of lotion, 'painted' each of us all over, with an emulsion brush, before we put on fresh nightwear. We had no bathroom, just a long tin bath which was brought in from outside where it hung on the wall. Gallons of hot water had to be heated so that the five of us could bathe before the medication routine, and there was no washing machine to do all the bedding and nightwear.

Having our grandparents as neighbours was quite significant, although the relationship was not a close one. Our uncle was working in a local colliery and this frequently involved night shifts. Grandma was constantly on at us about one thing or another: 'Remember your uncle is in bed', or 'Don't play with those balls banging up the wall' and 'If you go down the entry with those roller skates on you will wake your uncle'. He seemed to me to sleep like a log but Grandma always had some remark to make.

Uncle would wind her up. I was learning to play the recorder and he particularly enjoyed 'Greensleeves', one of the tunes in my music book. He would ask specifically, 'Greta, play "Greensleeves" to me.' But after I had played just a few notes Grandma would call, 'Will you stop that row?' I couldn't do right for doing wrong and didn't know whose instruction I was supposed to heed.

As siblings we children argued, but we were also great companions. The three girls in the middle of the family, of whom I was the youngest, spent a lot of time together. We each had a pair of roller skates and so we choreographed dances and practised routines. We spent hours in the local recreation ground, not only playing on the 'legitimate' swings, slide, etc., but also adventuring further onto the fields where there was an old clay pool we called 'the cloddies'. By today's standards it was very dangerous indeed, but we looked out for one another and fortunately we never came to any harm.

The period immediately following my birth had been very significant, with serious long-term implications for me. No-one could ever have known just how my life would be affected by a decision taken in the first few weeks of my life.

My mother had become seriously ill with septicaemia. Babies are now born into aseptic environments, onto sterile paper towels, with autoclaved instruments to deal with the umbilical cord, and then handled with great care by masked and rubber-gloved midwives. But I was born into an already busy household where housework was not top of the agenda, and maybe there should have been a little more preparation of the 'birth room'. Having said that, it is not clear where Mum came into contact with such a vicious strain of bacteria, but the impact was life-threatening.

Dad became deeply concerned and took on the role of carer, nursing Mum day and night and giving her the pre-scribed medication. Mum recognised the seriousness of the situation and became pragmatic even in illness. She decided what should happen to me if the rampaging infection could not be stopped and ended up taking her life.

My mum was a Christian, although she had drifted from her faith for a number of years. She had made a commitment when she was a teenager and had been an ardent follower of Christ. But at a time when she was not actively living out her faith, when God was on the back-burner of her life, she met and married my father who was not a Christian.

My dad was originally married to my mum's best friend. After only three years however his first wife died. They had no children. Because Mum knew him well and had in fact been a bridesmaid at the wedding, she began to visit Dad after work to cook his evening meal – the start of a beautiful friendship! After six months of this arrangement Dad thought it would be a good idea if they got married. So Mum had been bridesmaid and was now bride to the same man!

A number of years later Mum renewed her commitment to God and began attending church. At that time Dad didn't go to church and had no personal faith, but Mum attended a church that was not far from our home, just a short walk in the direction of the town centre. We children went along too.

Mum was outgoing and friendly and knew a number of people in the congregation. She was friendly with one particular woman with a history of not being able to carry a pregnancy to term. This woman had lost a number of pregnancies without ever having had a live baby. Mum decided that, if the worst came to the worst and the septicaemia was fatal, I should be given to this woman, Velma, and her husband, Roy, as they still had no children.

It is difficult to imagine Mum's thought processes or to analyse her reasons for making the choice she did. It may simply have been the ethos of the day. Although she told me this story herself, I have often wondered since whether Dad had any part in such a major decision. Was he even consulted, or was he just told? Did he object or did he think it was just not worth discussing? Did he protect and cherish me as his new baby? Did he verbalise any of his thoughts? Or did he give in to my mother?

But it was not to be. Mum recovered. I am very grateful to God, for reasons that will soon become obvious. However, the plan to give me as a baby to this particular couple brought the two women together as friends rather than just acquaintances in the same church.

My father was an emotionally distant figure, although there were times when we seemed to connect. When I was quite young I would look out for him coming home up the road from work on his bicycle. I would be sitting on the garden wall at the front of the house, watching and waiting. As he came over the hill and began cycling up the last stretch, I would run to meet him. He would put me on the crossbar for the last few yards and I would cling on tightly till we got home. Then I would often ask, 'Have you got anything for me?' and sometimes he had a sandwich left over from his lunch. It tasted delicious after it had been a day in Dad's bag, getting all squashed and squidgy. It was sometimes pork dripping, or lard and salt!

Dad would lie on my bed at night singing ditties before I went to sleep: 'Well I never, did you ever, see a monkey dressed in leather?' and 'Pardon, Mrs Arden, there's pigs in your back garden.' If any of us mentioned to Dad that we had a sore throat he would give us mashed butter and sugar, which he would prepare and bring to us in bed as a panacea. Amazingly it worked for us though it was not a medical textbook remedy, and we were never off school with a sore throat!

Although he lived in our house, slept in the matrimonial bed and worked to support the family financially, my father was not given to chit-chat. He didn't join in the games of Monopoly, challenge us to draughts or play cricket in the yard like Mum did. He would escape to the kitchen with his radio or take refuge in the garden or on his allotment. He was a stable man who provided for his family to the best of his ability, but had few skills in nurturing, encouraging or interacting with others. He had scant experience of parenting as he had left his own family home at about the age of fourteen following a family disagreement.

Dad worked hard. He loved gardening and, as I've said, produced mountains of fruit and vegetables for his family. He never took days off work right until the last two or three years before he retired. And he did weekend overtime to make ends meet.

My mother was Dad's complete opposite. She enjoyed company and sought people out. She would socialise rather than keep the home going and was generally considered to be a neighbourly person. We lived in a street where people knew everybody, chatted across garden walls and kept an eye out for one another. Mum was in her element.

Mum was a happy, chirpy character who came across as being capable and resourceful. She was the nurturer and the affectionate one. I remember kneeling on the floor as she sat in a chair and hugging her as I laid my head on her ample breast. Each time I left the house I kissed her.

Mum was the one who would listen to my spellings and times tables. She was the one who would glance over my shoulder at my homework. She knew how to repair the zip on my pencil case. When I became an adult, that perception of her competence remained with me. If I was finding a knitting pattern difficult, if I needed help in decorating a room, if I needed advice on cooking, Mum would be there as a safety net.

As a young child I remember neighbours popping in, or Mum and I would go to their homes. It was friendly and gossipy, and I enjoyed it. This kind of visiting became the norm with Velma and Roy too, although they were not immediate neighbours but lived a few streets away. We went to their house on innumerable occasions, although strangely our visits were rarely reciprocated.

Velma and Roy did not remain childless. They adopted a small girl called Ann. Because I was the youngest girl in our family I was the nearest in age to Ann who was two years my junior. The two mothers thought it would be good if, while they were chatting and having their cups of tea, Ann and I would play together. It was a perfect arrangement. They were happy and the children were happy.

Velma and Roy lived in a house with a greenhouse at the back, beyond the lawn, where the garden furniture sat. While running around the greenhouse at Ann's birthday party one day, I slipped on some damp grass. Putting my hand out to save myself from a fall, I steadied myself on the glass of the greenhouse, but the force of the impact caused the pane to shatter. I sustained a cut about four inches long, which required nine or ten stitches. I was seven at the time.

Their house had a similar number of rooms to ours but they also had a bathroom. There was a tiny kitchen with a free-standing larder cupboard with a drop-down worktop. And this was the house where my childhood started to become distorted.

One day Ann and I were playing in the garden. We were both small and, as Ann was younger than me, I took charge as we tried to erect a deckchair. Even adults find this difficult. Working out which part of the frame stays on the level and which is the back rest is the first challenge. Exactly how do the frame and canvas make anything resembling a structure that is safe to sit in? As two little girls we stood no chance of being able to fathom this oversized puzzle. But we pressed on, putting the chair this way and that, though we couldn't manage to get it into any recognisable shape.

Then the inevitable happened. Little fingers got trapped in the wooden frame. Ann shrieked and cried as she felt two of the pieces of wood pinching and trapping her small digits.

Velma and Roy were inside, but as soon as they heard their daughter's cries they appeared on the lawn. I fled. I don't remember any words; I just knew it would be best if I disappeared so I could get away from the anger that was now very evident. I ran from the lawn, across the patio area and through the gate, and was just making my way across the front garden when I was caught. I was distraught.

Roy took me back into the house and Velma decided that the seriousness of this event called for an aspirin. I have never understood the basis for that decision: why should a small sobbing child need to be medicated? However, I did as I was told and swallowed the aspirin. After all, I always did what I was told.

Velma and Roy seemed in a panic. They could not possibly let me go home in a distressed state, because if I told about the deckchair, who knew what else I might say? Would other things that went on in that house come out too? Would I find the words and courage to be able to tell my parents?

The attention had a calming effect, and eventually I was allowed to go home.

The visits continued but I knew that something was not right. Once I was standing right by the open doorway into their sitting room. On the opposite side of the room was a sofa where a girl wearing plaid trousers was crouched down on her knees. On her left, facing me, I noticed that the side zip of her trousers was undone. A man was behind her, seated on the sofa but at an angle and with his arms around her waist. I couldn't see his hands. It looked like a play fight but the girl was very determined. She stayed curled up, head in the cushions of the sofa, her back arched like a cat's. I heard noises. Was she distressed? Was she laughing? Was he cajoling her? I didn't know. Roy was inflicting what I am now certain was a sexual act on one of my sisters.

2 'Children should be seen and not heard'

We never had enough money to go round but we made our own fun. And we enjoyed occasional family days out visiting cousins and friends. That was the extent of our social life but we were happy.

There were times when we did not get enough care and attention from our parents but we survived. And we received harsh physical punishment from Mum which we found humiliating.

Two of my older sisters and I loved swimming at an outside pool. As I mentioned earlier, Dad bought us a season ticket each for several years. This meant we could make as many visits as we liked during the summer months. I learned to swim from a combination of spending so much time in the pool and lessons at school. I entered inter-school galas and won certificates. The sense of achievement was wonderful.

At school I knew that there were many children who had much more than we had, but there was also the odd family that was worse off. There were some things that I found embarrassing about our circumstances and poverty, and it was hard for me to deal with this.

We attended Sunday school and took part in 'the sermons', an annual event in the church calendar. We wore new outfits and the three youngest girls were dressed alike. We often performed a poem or some kind of recitation in front of church members and parents.

On one occasion there were some special evangelistic meetings. The date was 29 July 1959 and I was only seven but I realised that the man preaching was speaking to me. He told of Jesus dying on the cross. He explained the significance of this momentous event. He described how the wrong we have all done has separated us from God, who hates sin. But he also said that a relationship with God is possible when we truly believe and trust God to forgive our sins. I believed and invited God to come into my life.

We weren't allowed to go to the cinema, attend dances, wear make-up or go to parties. On Sundays we went to church for morning and evening services and in between we were not permitted to play outside. We had to stay indoors, occupying ourselves to pass the time.

But the things that were going on in another part of my life were far more destructive to me than any of the limitations placed on me at home. It had begun at a very young age and I was conditioned to accept it as part of my life: I was being systematically sexually abused. By the time I was seven I had very uncomfortable and frequent abdominal pain. My body and emotions were crying out against what was happening and I had irritable bowel syndrome.

I visited Velma and Roy's house literally hundreds of times during my childhood and teenage years. Initially I was accompanied by Mum, but as I grew older I was invited alone. I would play and then stay for tea. I slept at their home twice a week for about two years and went on at least four holidays with them. Ann and I were thrown together because of our mothers' friendship.

But although these invitations were to play, sleep over or visit Ann's grandparents, Roy never missed an opportunity to abuse me. He was desperate to get his hands on me. He followed me round the house, sat by me on the sofa, trapped me in corners or corridors, and tucked me into bed. Every move I made, he was behind me.

Sometimes he would wake me in the night. The family moved into a bigger house shortly after my accident in their garden. The new house had three bedrooms and was generally much bigger than the previous one. Ann and I would always sleep together when I stayed over. We had the choice of squashing into Ann's single bed in her room near her parents, or we could use the double bed in the spare room at the rear of the house. We used both.

One night in the rear bedroom I woke up suddenly. The house was quiet. Ann lay asleep on my left and I opened my eyes. The landing light was on. I didn't move. I felt cold and gradually my consciousness began to register what was happening. Gently I rolled my head from the left so that I could see in front of me. In the half light I saw Roy sitting on the bed. The bedclothes were thrown to one side of me while still covering Ann. Roy didn't notice I was awake.

I was terrified. Should I shout or scream? Would it be best if I jumped up and out of bed? I began to ask myself, 'Where's Velma? Is she asleep? Does she know he's here?' I felt trapped. I couldn't go anywhere because it was night. I had no-one to whom I could turn. No-one would believe me. I figured out that the best thing I could do was to act as if nothing had happened. I moved my legs and turned over as if still asleep. Roy got the message and left.

The single bed was a squeeze but sometimes I felt safer in there because Ann and I would huddle together. We lay giggling but apprehensive, listening for footsteps on the stairs. One of us would whisper to the other, 'He's coming, he's coming.' We didn't talk about what happened but Ann seemed aware of it. Roy would come into the bedroom. Sometimes Velma was with him but she would leave soon after kissing us goodnight. While pretending to straighten the sheets or tuck in the bedclothes, Roy's hands would instantly go under my nightdress.

There was an accompanying emotional numbness while all this was taking place, especially when I was in bed. I would distance myself from what was going on. Often I 'left my body' and rose to the ceiling. From this vantage point I could watch what was happening. I tried to be rational: 'But that's not me; I'm up here.' My childish mind was unable to comprehend it and my brain refused to process any emotions. But each time it happened the emotion was building. There were layers, one on top of another, week by week, year on year, creating a large volcano. I was unaware of any feelings, but my mind was storing them all up.

One day I came in from school to find that a piano had appeared in our house. I couldn't believe it; I was so surprised. It stood in the front room. It was shiny, new and a reddish mahogany colour. Until that moment I had had no idea that Mum could play the piano. I was overjoyed. Immediately I wanted to touch the keys and hear the amazing sounds they made. I was hooked!

Playing the piano became the first love of my life. I sat in the front room playing for many hours. I never had lessons but my gift astounded people. As I played I lost myself in the chords, the variety of sounds and all the cadences. And I often sang along. There were a number of songbooks that Mum used, so I knew many of the songs from hearing her play and sing them. There were hymns and there was a large brown book full of 'community songs'. My voice would burst forth with lyrics about darling Clementine, going over the sea to Skye, 'He walks with me', Christmas carols and so much more. The front room was not particularly inviting as it was cold, so more often than not I was alone as I played and sang. I had entered another world.

Not everyone shared my enthusiasm for the piano. My oldest sister would complain, 'Mum, can't you tell her to stop making that noise?' as the music reverberated into the next room. But for me it really was another world. I enjoyed being alone. The music was soothing. I felt a great sense of satisfaction. And it was also a spiritual experience. There was no other physical person in the room but I felt a presence with me.

I told no-one about the horrible things I was experiencing. Never for one moment did I consider telling a soul. Everything militated against it. I had no knowledge of words to describe body parts and I knew that nobody would believe me. Added to this was an innate certainty that I would not be able to address this taboo subject, for no-one ever spoke to me about sexual matters. The two separate tracks of my life in two different houses continued, but sometimes the influence of one track had an impact on the other.

There were two particular girls in our street with whom I sometimes played. It was always at their houses as we never invited children back to ours. Often when I was with each of them separately our play turned to pretend games about relationships. I was always the man. We were a couple. I began to act out with my friends the things that were happening to me.

School had both ups and downs but was relatively happy. I attended several sessions with a speech therapist in my early years to help with quite a pronounced lisp. I learned to play the recorder with Miss Aitken, who was young, attractive and very talented. During assembly I loved to listen as she played the piano. I wanted it to carry on. But sometimes it was Mr Lane who played and his style just wasn't the same. My numeracy skills were appalling but I loved everything to do with the English language. Words were fascinating and I enjoyed using them in a wide variety of contexts. So writing, spelling and reading were no hardship. Exercises of comprehension and précis were sometimes challenging but no less enjoyable. History did not capture my imagination at all. But geography with all its maps, colours, profiles of countries and loads of other interesting details gripped me.

But I struggled in other areas of school life. I was generally quite fearful of the adults around me. Teachers were not people to interact with; I spoke when I was spoken to and not before. I had very little confidence and was even afraid of some of my fellow students. I always handed homework in on time, had only one detention in six years of grammar school, and was never in trouble.

My school attendance record was exemplary, for I was hardly ever off ill. However no-one there knew a thing about the abuse I endured. Often on a Tuesday and Thursday I would walk from school to Velma and Roy's, have tea and stay the night. Back at school the following morning I looked exactly the same but only I knew the ghastly secrets of the time in between.

I went on my first holiday with Velma and Roy when I was ten. My teacher was not at all pleased that my mum had requested some time off during the autumn term. This was my final year and the emphasis was on training us all to pass the 11+ exam. Nevertheless Mum decided that I could go on holiday and so off I went to Blackpool for a week to see the illuminations.

We stayed in a rather shabby guest house not far from the promenade. We sampled all the usual holiday activities: trams, the fairground and the beach. Then there were the evening walks to see the grand display of lights. I loved the colourful characters and the pictures that shone out in the dark. There was so much to see that I didn't know which side of the road to look at first. We walked along trying to take it all in, with Ann and me jumping up and down shouting, 'Look at that one!' or 'Have you seen that?' But after the excitement it was back to the guest house for bed.

It was in Blackpool that I was introduced to two very peculiar customs. When we got back from our walk on the blustery promenade one night I was given a sugar lump soaked in brandy on a spoon to warm me up. How I hated the crunchy sugar. This was followed by a spoonful of liquid paraffin. Even worse. I gagged. It tried to force its way back up but I swallowed hard and was relieved that I managed not to vomit. These were new ideas. I pulled faces and tried to avoid the spoon but I had to take it. However, after that week I was never again forced to take the two dreaded spoons of 'medication'.

When I was about nine years old there had been a change in our church arrangements. I had been attending with my mother and sisters but Velma, Roy and Mum came to a decision. They were going to leave the church and start another one of a different denomination.

Life was hectic, acquiring a building for the new church, doing alterations and decorating and providing furnishings and all the things a small church needed. Although I was young I wanted to help. I varnished the chairs and had a go with an emulsion brush. I enjoyed it.

But, significantly, the new arrangements meant that the man who was abusing me was now my pastor.

One weekend there was a convention planned in a hired hall only a few yards from Velma and Roy's house. The guest speaker was their friend, a pastor in a town about twenty-five miles away. He was late in arriving. Someone asked me to go back to the house to see if he had arrived and if so to show him round to the hall. He was there, so with the key I had been given I let him in to deposit his overnight bag. Once inside the house he took hold of me, and with my arms hanging limply by my sides he kissed me on the lips in a very adult fashion for several seconds. Then we proceeded to the meeting as though nothing had happened.

The confusion and shock were traumatic. Why were all

these things happening to me? Was he going to involve me in anything else? I stood for a moment feeling very uncomfortable. Nothing more developed, but I felt deeply ashamed and embarrassed.

In addition to holidays and Tuesday and Thursday visits, I often visited Velma and Roy on Sundays when I was one of three regular visitors for lunch. The others were an older couple from our new church who lived some miles away. I was really interested in watching the developing relationships. We would sit at the dining table for a considerable time following the meal, the adults chatting and me listening intently. They often discussed the Bible and their views on certain doctrinal issues. But always for me there was something that spoiled the day.

I would help with jobs such as laying and clearing the table and washing dishes. This house had a walk-in pantry with shelves lining the walls, full of tins and packets of dried food. It also housed enamel baking dishes, crockery of all shapes and sizes, and cutlery. There was a shopping bag or two, and odd things that just found their way in there such as a magazine or a hair slide.

We used to come into the house following the church service. Velma would call to Roy, 'Put the kettle on, love.' Guests would then be served with drinks, Velma would be busy in the kitchen, still chatting away, and I would be laying the table. As I walked into the pantry the cutlery was on a shelf right opposite me and I would begin to count out the place settings. Someone would follow me in and stand right behind me. The door remained open, but with Roy's back to the door blocking me from view, no-one giving a cursory glance would have noticed him doing anything amiss. I would freeze to the spot, staring down at my bundle of knives and forks, as I felt his arms around my waist and my dress being lifted. The hum of conversation would continue in the adjoining room. Nobody suspected a thing.

Many times I would be at the sink washing up and Roy would come in to dry the pots. He would stand right behind me and press his body into mine. He was a short man and I was tall for my age. I knew it was all wrong. I was frightened, and his actions paralysed me.

As I grew and developed into a young teenager, little changed. I was still in the grasp of the perpetrator. My emotions failed me by not registering the damage I was suffering. My body betrayed me as it became aroused by things that were happening. And my voice remained silent. There was no escape.

I began to be interested in boys. Within our church there was quite a large group of young people, and considerable interaction between us all. Some nights we would walk together to a house meeting or into town or through the park.

We went to youth rallies in a hired minibus or a coach or a van belonging to one of our church members. Such outings became the breeding ground for boy–girl friendships. We received no instruction about how to conduct ourselves other than knowing that sex was a 'no-no'. It was so unfair. I was already the recipient of unwanted sexual activity on the one hand, but it was strongly implied that sexual activity with a boyfriend was totally improper.

My experiences set me apart from the other girls. They would giggle about kissing and being invited out by boys, but my unspoken words were, 'You don't know anything yet.'

I knew the church stance on purity but there was also my secret. There were times when I would watch Roy on the platform. It seemed a world away from what I knew went on in his home. I couldn't weigh it up. One minute he was the pastor, but later in the day he would put God aside while he indulged himself and inflicted his crimes on me.

Unsolicited abuse had created in me a huge area of knowledge that was totally inappropriate for my age. But it also generated arousal. A huge landslide had been set in motion by Roy's actions. My relationships with boys were tainted and the physical aspects of relating to men would be difficult in the future.

3 'There's no-one as happy as us'

One summer evening our school choir had a party. I had to ask Mum if I could go. She asked me all the ins and outs: 'Who will be there? What time does it start? When will you be home? Why do they have to have a party?' Finally I prised from her the permission I so desperately wanted.

But in spite of my keen desire to go, I didn't enjoy it at all. I was like a fish out of water. I didn't know the pop songs and felt socially inept, not knowing the norms. Nothing had prepared me for this kind of occasion. It was my first and last attempt to fit into any such school or social activities.

But even though it was hard, I had a small group of girl-friends to whom I felt I could relate. We laughed a lot together and we would meet up to walk to school and back. I began to gain confidence and was quite outgoing with a small select number of my classmates. One of my form teachers wrote on my report, 'A happy girl, but about time she settled down to some work.' I smiled a lot but underneath I was hiding my pain.

By the time I was fifteen I had been out with some of the boys from our youth group. But Velma and Roy even entered that area of my life too.

After we had been seeing each other for a number of months, my then boyfriend, Clive, moved about eighty miles away with his family. Velma had a longstanding friend who was pastor of a church in the town to which Clive had moved. She put them in touch with each other and expected Clive to attend the friend's church.

Clive and I wrote regularly, but we were young and of limited means and had no plans to visit each other. Velma received the news that Clive was not attending church and she duly passed this information on to my mother. The women decided that I would have to finish the friendship. Mum was in Velma's house and I was summoned into the room. Velma told me that because Clive was not attending church I must stop writing, and I wasn't to see him again.

I was devastated but I had no option. They said, 'There are plenty more fish in the sea.' No comfort or empathy. Velma's word was law. Mum accepted her stance on the matter. Together, the two of them were a force to be reckoned with.

Reading and rereading Clive's letters were my only comfort. I walked down the street thinking that he would step off a bus or come walking towards me. I daydreamed that a car would pull up and out he would step. I was trying to deal with a huge sense of loss all alone. It haunted me and I kept the letters for comfort.

This new trauma was added to my life while the abuse was continuing regularly. The injustice of it all began to dawn on me: 'How can this be happening? Roy can do just what he likes to me, but I can't even have a boyfriend of my choice.' I had no-one to whom I could express any of this.

But I began to develop a feistiness that I had not dared to express before. The abuse of many years was taking its toll and my attitude towards Roy was beginning to change. Up till then I had been fearful, compliant and lacking in confidence with adults. Disdain of Roy began to grow and soon it became a protective measure that spurred me into action.

I was becoming wise to his strategies and so I developed effective countermeasures. If he was alone in the kitchen I stayed out of it. If he called to me I would pretend not to hear. If Velma asked me to do something that involved being near to Roy, I gave him a wide berth. When he reached towards me I dodged his grasp.

I noticed that their relationship was of the 'hen-pecked' variety and took some comfort from the fact that he didn't always get his own way.

From then on there was no more physical contact with him but I was aware at times of him looking at me. He would make a twitching movement with his leg, lick his lips and leer. It was creepy but I was winning.

When I was sixteen I was in the middle of studying for 'O' levels. I had a considerable amount of homework so I sat at the dining table for many hours with books spread out, lists of tasks in my homework diary and the contents of my pencil case scattered all around.

Mum had been to a meeting one night and returned with some interesting news.

'I met a nice young man at church tonight. He's just moved to the area.' I showed a slight interest but carried on with what I was doing. Three years later I was married to the 'nice young man'.

Ian was my complete opposite. He was quiet and reserved, not given to much chit-chat, but we spent time together leading a small group of older children in our church. It was while we were in the church kitchen making refreshments one evening that Ian approached me and we kissed. We didn't say a word but instinctively I knew we would marry.

While we were dating, Ian and I had a few conversations about what had happened to me in my earlier years. Velma and Roy had been very supportive to Ian on moving into the church and so his perception of them was completely different from mine. Our conversations were very matter of fact, with no emotion attached.

There was one thing of which I was sure. I told Ian, 'I don't want Roy to marry us.' I repeated this many times but my confidence had not grown to the extent where I could do anything constructive about it, and neither had Ian's. He had experienced a very different Roy and Velma and couldn't equate the two versions. And having heard only the bare bones of what had happened to me, he was at a distance from my experiences. I knew there was no way I could persuade Roy or my mum that I wanted to be married by another minister. Ministers were held in high esteem and considered to be pillars of the community. Even as a young adult preparing for marriage I was 'doing as I was told'. It was expected that Roy would take the service, for after all he was the pastor. And take the service he did when we married in 1971.

Our first couple of years of married life were fraught with many arguments and battles. We both wanted our own way; both wanted to be the boss. I was away from the restrictive life I had lived, finding my feet, and determined that things would be how I wanted them to be.

After a year of marriage I embarked on the career I had always wanted. During my teenage years I had made occasional visits to our local hospital and talked with the matron. She had advised me on how I could prepare to go into nursing. Later I had applied to a large teaching hospital several miles away and decided to leave home and move into the nurses' home. But Dad said that he didn't want me to go. This was quite out of character and I didn't question him further. I actually felt quite honoured that he cared enough to want me to stay at home. He had never said that he loved me and hugs were not his way either. So this was a wonderful experience – Dad wanting me at home! I let the dream go.

Now that I was married I reapplied to a local teaching hospital and began training. I loved every minute although there were some definite challenges. The first time I injected someone I stood apprehensively at the washbasin in a large 'Nightingale' dormitory-style ward. I looked in the mirror and saw the drawn curtains around the waiting patient. There was a nurse tutor ready to supervise the big event, but the student nurse – me – was alas far from ready. I washed my hands extensively, wondering how long I could make this last and whether or not to run down the corridor. Finally I ventured behind the curtains and injected the patient with her pre-medication prior to surgery. I was on my way to becoming a nurse.

The role fitted me like a glove. I developed a love of people and talking with them. I was at ease while caring and discovered I had infinite patience within me. Marriage and nursing seemed to propel me forward with social skills and the ability to relate. I felt happy.

I worked on a ward with men who required medical nursing. Long-term patients were at the top of the ward, typically those recovering from strokes, while the acute patients were in sight of the office at the bottom.

Some of the men were really appreciative of receiving basic nursing care: help with shaving, support when walking, and the opportunity to get into a deep bath for a good soak. They often kept nurses talking, and friendships developed as patients stayed in hospital for a significant period of rehabilitation.

I had been talking with one particular man about when we were both children. During the conversation I told him that, although I had had a doll, I had no recollection of ever having had a teddy. Several days later a colleague was making his bed with another nurse and he asked her, 'Where's that other nurse?' In trying to define whom he meant he described me as 'You know, that one who's always smiling'. He gave me a soft honey-coloured teddy. That was a very special gift, although the giver never realised just *how* special.

As a couple we always enjoyed holidays. In May 1975 we were returning from a week in Cornwall and stopped at a National Trust property, making that day a part of the holiday too. We relaxed in the garden, pottered around admiring the colourful flowerbeds and ended up in the coffee shop.

We didn't go straight home as it was our plan to call on both sets of parents to let them know about our holiday. We arrived at Ian's parents and sensed that there was some tension in the air. Ian's mum, Del, asked, 'Have you been to see your mum yet?' I replied that we would be going to see her after our visit to them. I went into the lounge but unknown to me Del had signalled to Ian so he followed her into the kitchen.

Ian had to give me the shocking news that, just the evening before, my dad had died. He was only sixty-five and had been enjoying his retirement, but unfortunately it had been cut short.

I was angry. I thought about the lovely day we had enjoyed and the visits we had made on the journey back home. I wanted to know just why some inner feeling had not intimated to me that Dad had died. I felt guilty that I had been enjoying myself at such a crucial time when Dad had been in the process of leaving us all. I asked God, 'Why didn't you tell me?' And then my thoughts turned to Mum and I wondered, 'What do I say to my own mum when her husband has just died?'

So we went to see Mum. Several people had gathered in our family home. Unknown to us all, Dad had been living with high blood pressure that had never been treated, and he had suffered a haemorrhage, following which he had died within minutes. As I met Mum there was no need for words. We just embraced and for a while cried together.

In spite of all this we were settling into our marriage, and our Christian faith and commitment were growing. I had taken some young girls to a camp in south-west England and had a particularly joyful experience in my Christian faith. Ian was a keen Bible student, developing an extensive knowledge. After a few years we felt it was right for us to begin full-time Christian ministry and so we applied to the department within our denomination that focused on mission in the UK. They had a system of matching younger people with small, new churches across the UK. We were accepted.

We explored several possibilities and Ian and I visited the different towns. We wanted to see if any of them was to our liking. I was still nursing and so we also needed information about whether or not I would be able to continue my career.

The weekend visit we had made to see if one church was 'a fit' for us was astonishing in so many ways. The scenery was magnificent, the people so welcoming. Here was a picture-postcard town, and inside us we both felt a stirring of excitement.

Yet although we were certain that this was the place that God had directed us to, we hadn't committed ourselves immediately. We had felt we needed to talk together and pray and not be swayed by the charm and beauty of the area.

We were both giving up our jobs. This move would mean a change from a brand new house into an old shabby flat. There would be only a very limited income available to us from church funds. And our families would be quite a distance away. All in all there were several elements that could have been viewed as negative but we just knew it was right. The excitement remained with us and indeed increased as time went on. Ian phoned the pastor who had hosted our weekend visit and told him we wished to take up his offer.

So we moved in the spring of 1977 to North Yorkshire. This became our home for the next ten and a half years. We packed boxes, wrote our resignations and talked incessantly about the future. There were some practical glitches. The van didn't arrive, but after a four-hour wait and just a couple of hours in which to load our few belongings, we were off. We travelled north but again the van didn't arrive at the other end. We thought it would pull in behind us but it didn't. By now it was about six in the evening. We were left without a bed, a kettle or any of the basics until the following morning. But it didn't detract from our excitement and joy because we knew that what we were doing was right.

A couple of years before we moved, Velma and Roy had moved to another area of the country. Now we were living only about thirty-five miles away from them. We still had occasional contact and they came across to our induction service. They had been my mum's friends and I found it impossible to cut them off without a good reason. Neither would Ian cut them off because at that stage he had no real understanding of the impact of abuse and was far too loyal to do such a thing without good cause.

We decorated the flat, made it our own and were deeply happy there. While I was working in midwifery it had been common to chat with new mums and several had asked me the obvious: 'Have you got any children?' I would reply that we didn't particularly want any. But at Christmas 1977 Ian said, 'Let's have a baby.' We didn't have extended discussions or debates. I simply said, 'OK then', and in October the following year Adam was born.

There have been only a very few occasions that I would call 'life-changing'. Having children qualified. We had counted ourselves extremely happy before we had children. But our first child brought an extra dimension into our relationship. Not only were we a family, but we were experiencing an overwhelming love that we shared with this little person. In bed each night Ian and I would talk about the day. Our whole conversation would revolve around what Adam had done. We thrilled at his every smile, noted how much he had slept and the increasing time he spent awake, laughed at his antics and commented on how he was beginning to chuckle. We were the kind of doting parents who thought their baby was the only one in the world.

Adam was not an inquisitive toddler; he never emptied cupboards or bookshelves and he was content with his toys. We would play games together and read stories. We would take him to visit new people and places. He never made unreasonable demands. Life continued to be good.

Soon we moved from the flat into a lovely bungalow. This was only a short-term let and so we moved again, this time into an unusual apartment, part of a huge building, so old that it had a preservation order to keep the outside structure in its original form. But inside it had been gutted, renovated and made into homes for six families. We spent around six years there.

Music was a constant theme running through my life. When we married one of the first things I had had to have was a piano. I could not imagine being without one. I played a lot at home and also in church. I was invited to play at weddings and funerals, sometimes accompanying myself by singing too. The gift that had developed in my childhood became increasingly useful and I went on to play other instruments too.

I decided that I wanted not only to play by ear, but to be able to play by reading the music too. This would widen my skills and I could learn how to play classical pieces. So early each Saturday morning I took myself off to piano lessons. It was difficult initially to go back to playing simple tunes after having played well for most of my life, but I persevered. However, after a couple of years of working at it quite intensely, the lessons and exams were put on hold as our family expanded further.

After a miscarriage, and having waited a while, we knew we wanted to add to our family, and so Timothy was born in 1983. He was completely different from Adam in character and personality. Within just a few weeks of his birth I knew there was something amiss so I consulted the health visitor. Timothy would spend hours awake during the day, mostly crying. He had medication for colic, which helped a little, but as the months went on he was finally diagnosed as having allergies to various foods and additives. We changed the family diet completely and this made a huge impact on our lives and on Timothy in particular. He developed a very winsome and attractive personality and made us laugh. But he was always getting into mischief and was quiet only when listening to stories or when finally asleep at night. He needed a lot of attention. We were exhausted and at times frustrated, but we were happy.

Ian and I often used to comment that we thought there was no-one as happy as us. We loved each other, we had two beautiful boys, and we lived in a very picturesque part of the country. Financially we were often lacking, but in amazing ways we came through. Having settled some of Timothy's problems, we seemed to be coping with our family quite well. But I had had several siblings and felt it was not much of a family with only two children. I wanted more.

4 'But your eyes are not smiling'

In October 1985 my life took a serious and very significant turn. I was at home on my own for the weekend with the children. Ian had gone to a residential prayer conference sixteen miles away. The delegates had free time allocated on the Saturday afternoon, so I took the boys along and met up with Ian. The boys played on the swings and ran round the park with a ball. We joined in the fun but also chatted about how the weekend was going. There were one or two things I needed to buy so we went to the shops. Our own town was very small and limited so I took advantage of this bigger place.

We were standing in Woolworths.[1] The boys had chosen a small item each and I had some pegs in my hand. As we stood at the checkout waiting our turn, Ian said, 'Why don't I take the boys home and you can stay for the prayer meeting tonight?' In a matter of seconds I felt a huge grey cloud settle over me. 'I couldn't pray if I tried,' I replied. I drove the boys home. This was the beginning of a very dark period of four and a half years under that cloud.

Depression was not a word in my vocabulary. I was 'happy-go-lucky', the 'life and soul of the party'. Socially I had developed from suffering from teenage angst and a lack of confidence into someone who loved being hospitable and filling the house with people, chatting with anyone and everyone. There were toddler groups and a playschool in which I took an active part. We held discussion groups in our home with people from church. Depression? I had no room in my life for depression.

I was often tired from the demands made on me by family and church. I did not have enough time at home as I spent hours every day with Timothy walking and playing in parks in an attempt to keep him occupied. Occasionally I would say I was fed up, but depression was completely outside anything I had experienced. There was no terminology I could attach to my mood.

After Timothy was born I did have a very short period when I sometimes panicked and didn't like Ian to be out of my sight. We were renting an allotment and Ian found it relaxing tending to the plants, digging and harvesting crops. I hated it when he went even for a short while. But this passed. I knew that lots of people went through the baby blues and once I was over that episode I didn't give it a second thought.

But now my mood was very low indeed. It was difficult to communicate what was going on inside my head. The place where I found myself was a very dark one.

After a few weeks I discovered I was pregnant again. This was what I had wanted so much, more children, but now the timing seemed completely wrong. I began to wonder if I could cope, contemplated my struggle, and concluded that it would all be OK because surely I would be back to normal soon. But instead of getting better I got worse.

Ian and I were in the habit of waking early before the boys so that we could have some quiet time. We often followed the same pattern. Ian would walk by the boys' room quietly so that they would not be disturbed. Adam was a heavy sleeper but Timothy woke easily. It was important to let him sleep on as long as possible because, once his day had started, there was very little respite.

When downstairs Ian would make tea and bring a cup to me and then we would read our Bibles, me upstairs in bed and Ian downstairs in the sitting room. It was sometimes only a matter of minutes before I was being bombarded by a toddler running in to jump on the bed, but at other times I was able to enjoy my peace for a little longer.

It was during one of these early-morning times that I was reading from the story of Abraham. The context was about him moving house, and the version of the Bible I was reading said that Abraham went to 'the place where he first built an altar'. It struck me so forcibly that I wrote something in my Bible. This was quite out of character. When I wrote about things that I wanted to take note of I always wrote in a notebook, never in the Bible itself – my tidy mind wouldn't allow me to do that. However, such was the impact of the words that I wrote, 'We will move to the town where I was born and brought up.' Inside I knew that God was using this story to direct us, although it would be another two years before we actually moved. We had no thoughts of uprooting when I first read those words.

During my depression I was able to maintain our morning routine and sometimes I felt it gave me the strength to carry on. But often I was tearful and felt a deep despair. I had to push myself to carry on as usual because the boys, the church and my husband needed me – everyone wanted a part of me. I even had a very small part-time job in the village school. I had no concept of space for myself or taking time out to help my recovery. I just pushed on and on and on.

I had no idea why I was feeling so desperate. I felt guilty for being so weak and unable to cope. I felt a failure.

Apart from Ian, no-one knew what I was going through. The pregnancy progressed well initially. Adam went to school. Timothy started playgroup. I attended church, led the worship, talked with everyone. Outwardly life seemed quite normal. But inside I was dying.

I began to feel angry about the state I was in. Anger had been a problem for me for a long time. Usually I maintained an even keel for long periods and then I would explode over the smallest thing. But now this was anger with myself.

In my mind I began to rail at myself: 'I'm a Christian and I shouldn't be feeling like this.' This was usually followed by: 'Where is the victorious Christian life I should be living?' I was so confused. There were certain things I had been taught as a child growing up in church that I assumed were true and now my experience was telling me differently. The perspective of Christianity that I had imbibed was about being happy, avoiding the valley and living on the dizzy heights of the mountain. I couldn't work it out. My experience was far from the theory I had cherished. I was deeply disappointed with myself for not being a better Christian.

In around the thirtieth week of pregnancy my hormone levels began to show some erratic behaviour. I had to bring large urine containers home each week and collect twenty-four-hour samples for testing. Eventually, around five weeks before my due date, I was taken into hospital for rest as the baby was not thriving and my GP was concerned.

The bed rest was a real godsend. One of my sisters helped Ian by having Timothy for a few days, and a family in our church had Adam to stay and play with their boys several times. Staff then decided that I should have a Caesarean section as the baby was a breach presentation and they did not want to put him under any further strain. I had an epidural for the birth and was awake to see our third son placed in my arms.

But Nathan was not well, and shortly after our first cuddle he was whisked away to the special care baby unit. He spent the next two weeks being nursed, and once I was on my feet in the recovery period, the staff invited me to stay in hospital until he was ready to leave too. This would involve leaving the main ward and living in the mother-and-baby rooms in the special care unit. I was torn. I wanted to be with him. He was tiny, vulnerable and ill. But I had spent so many hours each day in that part of the hospital and it was not inviting. It had few windows and I was already depressed, added to which my hormones were now in a post-partum whirl.

I went home to be with the other two boys and Ian, but visited the hospital each day to feed and spend a few hours with Nathan. That year we postponed Timothy's third-birthday celebration and held his party two days later.

After daily round trips of fifty miles to the hospital we brought Nathan home and our family was finally together. I had some help over the next few weeks while I recovered from surgery. It was quite a positive time. Timothy looked forward to our helper arriving, and she would encourage him to take a duster and they would chat as they did jobs together. This gave me some vital time with Nathan during school hours, and then I was free to be with Adam after school.

Long before Nathan was born, while I was feeling well, I had thought that having two children was relatively easy. We had sorted out Timothy's diet and, although he was still extremely active and always needed to be occupied, at least the tantrums and screaming had stopped. But now I was far from well and two children plus one baby somehow didn't add up to three; it was more like a multitude of children.

I was sinking fast. My face was drawn, my eyes were hollow, my energy was at an all-time low and I felt that I could take no more. Through the haze of visits to the doctor and appointments with the health visitor, no-one picked up what was happening. At night I would fall into bed and sob quietly on Ian's chest: 'I don't want to wake up in the morning. I want to sleep for ever. I just want to die.'

Ian was very worried. The person he loved and had married wasn't there any more; she was an empty shell of her former self. He had no idea what to say or how to handle the situation. He would hold me as we lay together and pray. I cried myself to sleep many, many times.

Morning would come and I hadn't slept for ever. But the first few seconds of waking were delicious. I had no depression; I felt well and I looked forward to being with the children. But this was during the process of waking. Once my mind caught up with my body it all came flooding back. Another dark day in the deep pit.

It became clear to me that this was a mental illness; I was going mad. But if that was the case then I had a dilemma. I didn't do 'mental illness'. I was a Christian, in church leadership. Who on earth does a pastor's wife talk to about these kinds of things? I was tormented.

Adam was growing and developing an awareness of the fact that I was not as I had been. He was concerned about me, and I in turn was concerned about the impact of the depression on each of the children. One day Adam looked straight at me and asked, 'Are you alright, Mummy?' What could I say? I couldn't explain to an eight-year-old that I was depressed. I couldn't think of a way round it. I just wanted to reassure him that, even if I wasn't OK now, I would be in the future. I didn't want him to be frightened. I wanted him to feel secure and loved, but how could I convey all these things to him? So I just said quietly, 'Yes I'm fine.' Instantly he replied with a perception more mature than his years: 'But your eyes are not smiling.'

Ian and I were both becoming increasingly aware that our time in Yorkshire was coming to an end. This had not been on our agenda. We had thought we would be there for a long time, we loved the place, we had formed some wonderful relationships with people, the local school was good and we lived in an idyllic spot. But there was a growing inner sense of not being as settled as we had been. Thoughts that God perhaps wanted us to move on became more prominent.

The children went down with most of the usual childhood ailments but also more than their fair share of some. Adam was very prone to tonsillitis and suffered repeatedly during his first eight years. Timothy had many symptoms of hyper-activity, and Nathan had repeated ear infections, which on one occasion caused his eardrum to burst. The doctor came to know us very well. It was a small town so we were usually able to see the same person each time and we were on first-name terms. The doctor had visited the house after each of the children was born and he knew their history, and I had confidence in the care we all received.

I was back at the surgery once again, and talking about Nathan's symptoms which I recognised as signifying yet another ear infection. At that time I was not terribly self-aware and I knew little about body language. However, I had seen a couple of photos of myself and knew that I looked quite dreadful, with very dark, sad eyes and no smile. After checking Nathan's ears and confirming what I already knew, the doctor, Bob, talked through the treatment with me. Then Bob turned to me and asked, 'And how are *you*?' For just a second I was shocked. I hadn't intended talking about me. I had gone only to help Nathan. Why had he asked about me? Tears began to roll down my face. This was the first time I had been asked to talk about how I felt. I was touched and embarrassed but also relieved that I could unload a little.

I didn't say much. I wasn't used to this type of interaction. After all, I was usually the one who asked others how they were feeling. I described some of my symptoms briefly and said how confused I was by all that was happening. Bob listened and asked me a few questions about the type of support I was receiving and whether or not I had family who could help. I told him that my family were some distance away, but that we were considering moving and there was a distinct possibility that we would move nearer to them. He then asked me to come back and see him again, requesting that I book the last appointment of the morning so we could talk without the pressure of time and other waiting patients.

I returned a couple of weeks later without any of the children in tow and I took a notebook with me. I had started to write. An amazing journey of therapy had begun. No-one told me what to do or how to go about relieving some of my distress, but instinctively I wrote during many of my early-morning times alone. I never showed it to the doctor as it wasn't appropriate. The talking helped and I appreciated the time he gave me. I saw him only on a couple of occasions but it was enough to show me the value of talking to someone.

I continued to write. I didn't have that person whom I realised I needed, but writing became a substitute for talking. I expressed frustration about why I was in such a mess. I wrote about wanting to die and yet loving my children so much that I knew I wouldn't ever take that step. I wrote about my confusion about Christian doctrine and teaching. There was anger and yet I didn't really know why. I dabbed at the paper as it became damp with the tears dropping onto it.

The following weeks and months helped us to consolidate our thinking about whether we should move house or not. Ian was increasingly anxious about me. We were now certain that we would move. And despite attempts not to, we moved to the town where I had been born and brought up, just as God had impressed on me two years before as I had been reading my Bible. Both Ian's family and mine were still in the same area. We explored housing and schools, our two main priorities, and made firm plans.

We were now living in a large house and, with three children, it was quite a task to get packing organised, so I had deliberately started early. But there was still a huge amount to do and I was feeling the pressure. For two weeks one thought reverberated in my head over and over again: 'How will I ever pack up this house, how will I ever pack up this house, how will I ever pack up this house?' I was already exhausted and demotivated from my illness, and now I had a deadline to be out of the house, hand over the keys and leave the place in a reasonable state for the next occupant. It seemed impossible, but several people came to our rescue.

I had one very close friend, Sue, whom I had met at playgroup, and she helped with the packing. We had developed a deep friendship when her husband had been seriously ill and I had been able to mind her children while she visited the hospital. And now she was returning the favour. We were dreading the day when we would have to say goodbye but, unknown to me, in every box she packed she placed a small handwritten note. These were delightful to find at the other end when those same boxes were unsealed.

A few male members of the wider family came up for the move. They hired a large van and camped overnight in our house, surrounded by all our packing. They loaded it all up the next day and drove to our new home.

A church friend came on the day of the move to clean the house. As soon as a room had been cleared, there she was with the vacuum cleaner, dusters and damp cloths making sure it was as clean as a whistle.

The boys were amazing. One night they were in Yorkshire, the next night they were much further south, but they never looked back. There were no troubled nights. Adam was starting a new school, Timothy was about to start school, and Nathan was now fifteen months old.

It was traumatic for Ian and me. We hadn't made a conscious decision to return to my home town, but this was the only door open to us. It was not a happy time for either of us, and for me the move only added to the depression.

5 'What has happened to you?'

We unpacked with lots of help from our families. I tried to direct operations so that boxes and furniture went into the right rooms. The boys were excited to see their new bedrooms, the garden and especially the play area further down the close.

The extended family stayed on after the initial flurry, by which time we were all getting hungry. There was no way in which I was about to start preparing food after a day of packing and unpacking on top of a long journey. So someone went along to the local chip shop, returning with takeaways. We sat wherever we could find a spot and ate together.

The house was just what we wanted in so many ways, with enough room for living and several storage areas too. It was a good design for a family and it caught the sun almost all day. Ian had prayed that we would have a bright house with plenty of opportunity to enjoy the sun. He felt that God had given him just what he wanted.

The garden was a novelty for the children. Our previous house had had only a parking space and little else. The boys loved being outside in all weathers. They had the rest of the summer to enjoy, and often played with water pistols or water balloons or on bikes and scooters. Later in the year they would wrap up and play for short bursts, coming in periodically to get warm before putting on all their outdoor stuff again and going back out.

Then there was the school term to think about. Timothy was due to start and Adam had a place at the local middle school, just five minutes' walk away. Before leaving Yorkshire I had written to the two schools nearest our new address. One had replied and allocated a place to Adam. The school for younger children had not made contact, so we didn't know whether Timothy had a place or not.

I took Adam to school and settled him in before walking to the primary school with Timothy. But this school was full. However, the head teacher recommended another one about two miles away, where Timothy began to attend mornings only.

Ian started work in a church which had invited him to join the leadership team. It was a big church with a wide range of activities each day. Ian began to find his feet and enjoy his new role, although leaving Yorkshire had been a great wrench for us all.

Everyone was busy getting on with all their new challenges while Nathan and I struggled together at home. He was deeply affected by my depression. He needed lots of comfort and it seemed to me that I was depressing him. The guilt of this depressed me even further. He clung to me, he seemed unhappy and he showed little interest in his toys. At the end of each day I would often think to myself, 'What has he played with today?' One of my strategies for coping with his dejection and misery was to give him a bath, usually during the afternoon. This helped in many ways. While in the water, Nathan wasn't sad or grumpy. He loved the bubbles and bath toys. And for me it was a manageable option. I could sit on the floor splashing around with him and it made no real demands on me.

One Sunday morning about two years after the move, we attended our usual church service. Mum went to the same church as us, and after the service she wasn't feeling well and told me that she was going home. Normally she stayed and chatted with people, so I knew that she really wasn't feeling well if she wasn't up to this. Mum lived next door to one of my sisters so I immediately phoned her. 'Mum's coming home; she doesn't feel well. Could you get the doctor, and I'll be with you as soon as I can?' Later we called at Mum's and found the doctor leaving the house. We took the prescription and collected Mum's medication, taking it straight back to her so that she could start treatment. As soon as she had taken some tablets I said goodbye and left her in bed to rest. I knew that my sister would look in on her and prepare food when she was ready to eat.

Later that afternoon when I saw Mum again it was such a shock: following a phone call informing me of her sudden death. Apparently her heart had become tired and given up. I was shaken but the over-riding feeling was that of being abandoned. Although I still had my husband and children, I felt like an orphan. This fuelled my illness and complicated my feelings, feelings that were a whole new area for me. Before the four years of depression I would have described myself as consistent and happy, with the occasional out-burst of anger. Although I had lost Dad and Grandpa, I had experienced some sadness but no real grief. I always got over things and reverted to my smiley self with a business-as-usual attitude to life.

But now I was in a real fix. I cried so much I couldn't identify what I was crying about. Was this something in the present? Was it a reaction from the past? There seemed to be so many tears to cry, about so many things, and now I was bereft of Mum too.

There seemed no hope that things would ever get better. However, amazingly, a change was just around the corner.

One weekend in the spring of 1990 the cloud lifted. By Sunday lunchtime I noticed that there had been an improvement over the previous twenty-four hours. Ian and I were in the kitchen preparing vegetables for the Sunday roast. My neck and shoulders, which had so often been tense and painful, had improved significantly, and during the morning I realised that the tension had gone completely. I felt reluctant to speak about it because I was afraid it would only be short-lived. But it was not only the pain that had gone; my mood was considerably lighter. As we worked together I said to Ian, 'I think it's gone.'

And it had. Almost as quickly as it had come the cloud went. I was so happy. Free at last! I began to look for part-time work. The old me was back, my energy levels soared and off I went again at full pelt.

What a difference! I was no longer feeling sad all the time. I was able to care for the children and even became involved as a volunteer in some activities in school. I was attending church and heavily involved in the music ministry and weekly practices.

Although I felt good, I was puzzled. I couldn't for the life of me understand what the last four and half years had been about. Why had I, an optimistic and usually buoyant, happy-go-lucky person, been through such a prolonged depression that had no obvious cause?

I loved having the children and they had been my only joy during the depression, but now it had gone they were an even greater joy to me. We did things together. I planned school holidays to include activities that they would all enjoy. On long car journeys, especially going on holiday, I would create games and quizzes. Being a mother was so much richer now that I had three lovely children and no depression to hamper me.

It was April and I was newly released from the cloud. As a church we were making preparations for Easter. Part of the plan was to hold an outdoor service in the town centre on Good Friday. Ian and I attended with the boys.

Although we had been in the church for over two years, because it was so big there were obviously some people whom we knew better than others. One particular family had invited us to their home for a meal. They too were at the outdoor service. At the end Dot came up to me and asked, 'What has happened to you?' I was thrilled that there was such an obvious change. I knew that I felt so different but for someone to comment on it was wonderful. I replied, 'Can you tell?' and then I went on briefly to describe that I had been depressed and just a couple of weeks earlier it had lifted. She invited me to their new house, as they had moved since we had eaten together. That was the start of a great friendship and a new spiritual dimension to my life.

Dot and I prayed together each Monday morning. On one of these occasions we were sitting outside and I was talking to her about my concerns for Nathan due to my earlier depression. As he was still not at school I usually took him along with me when I saw Dot, and so while he was pottering around the garden she prayed over him that there would be no lasting ill effects in his life. Following this he went on to develop interests and eventually started school quite confidently and happily.

I was not successful in obtaining a part-time job. As I was at home much of the time I decided that, instead of making more applications and having to deal with continual disappointment, I would get a dog. Before we had children we had had several cats, and continued to have over the years, but we had never had a dog. I broached the subject with Ian and his only stipulation was 'OK, but let's not have a big one.' I took myself off to the RSPCA kennels and chose a beautiful dog, returning a couple of weeks later to introduce the family to her. We had to wait a while as she was weaning puppies, but soon we were able to bring

Polly home with us. Walking with her was to become hugely important to me.

About a year after Mum died we heard that Velma was ill. Over a period of years our contact with Velma and Roy had dwindled to just a Christmas card and a very occasional phone call. Ian went to visit Velma when she was ill and it was not long before she too died. It was much later that I would recognise the significance of having neither Mum nor Velma as part of my life.

I had been depression-free for about fifteen months. But then we were hit by a fresh storm. Ian had always been quite melancholic by nature and this meant he was prone to low moods and feelings. While I was depressed he did an admirable job of keeping himself together and not putting me under further pressure, but he couldn't withstand another blow.

As I said, he was in team ministry at church. However, after almost five years there were funding problems and the department in which Ian worked closed down. He was now unemployed. This was a completely new experience. Ever since leaving school he had always had a job, and after fifteen years of full-time ministry we were both wondering what the next step could be. We discussed options. I made suggestions. Ian went to the job centre and bought the local paper to see what vacancies were around. After only two weeks he became very downhearted, recognising even more that he was the type of person who needed to be working.

Having few formal qualifications to equip him for the secular world, Ian decided to go to the local college for a year's intensive study which would qualify him for university. He was now occupied and motivated, but at the same time feeling extremely disappointed that his ministry seemed to be at an end. He had good days and bad, but I was there to support him.

About this time we had to make what I can only describe as another traumatic decision. Ian and I had both been Christians for many years. Attending church and sharing fellowship and friendship with other Christians was top priority in our lives. The only reason we had ever left a church was because we had moved house. We had never chosen to leave a church just to have a change or on a whim. But because Ian had been made unemployed by the church, this had an impact on his role in leadership too. We were very uncomfortable. People were beginning to ask questions that we felt it was not our responsibility to answer. We were loyal to the leaders and didn't want to say anything that would put our slant on issues and cause disruption. It became unbearable.

One Sunday morning we were sitting in church and the words of a very old hymn came to me:

> In simple trust like those who heard, beside the Syrian sea,
> The gracious calling of the Lord, let us like them without a
>   word
> Rise up and follow Thee, rise up and follow Thee.[1]

This was not a hymn we sang or used very often, but God seemed to highlight it to me in a way that confirmed that we should leave, and without trying to justify ourselves or explain things. So we just told the leaders that we would be leaving and left without speaking about the depth of our feelings.

We found another church which met in a local school not far from the school that Nathan and Timothy now attended. Adam was older and wanted to stay on at the previous church as he had friends of his age and was involved in the music group there. We agreed.

Although financially things were tight for us while Ian studied, we were managing to survive. The boys were happy and growing, with lots of friends and interests. I had started a part-time job.

We were settling well into our new church. I was playing the piano and getting more involved. Ian found it difficult as he had no particular role in church now, but he was busy with his studies and also trying to keep a lid on his hurt and trauma from the redundancy.

At home we had a succession of cats and two litters of kittens, which we all loved. The dog was becoming very much a part of the family and could be quite a handful at times, but everyone liked her. I took up piano lessons again and went on to do more grades.

And then, in spite of the unexpectedly painful episode with the social worker, our fostering application was successful too. We were thrilled, and only about three weeks after getting the go-ahead from the fostering panel our first beautiful baby arrived. The boys were excited to have a baby in the house. Adam would chat with the birth mother who often visited to see her little son. Timothy wanted to help with feeding and Nathan occasionally gave the baby a cuddle. Over a couple of years we had several babies for months at a time until their destiny was decided and they went off to other families.

Since the social worker's visit during which I had grieved my lack of birthday parties I had sometimes wondered why my distress had been quite so profound. It was no big deal, just an occasional thought that would cross my mind and then go back into a quiet recess, not to be dwelt upon for a while.

Ian completed his year at college with distinctions in all his exams and proceeded to university. The journey there was long and the studying was challenging. But I helped him by reading through assignments and checking spelling and grammar. I made sure that the boys gave him the time he needed for studying, but there was no separate study and our sitting room also doubled up as the dining area, so Ian was sometimes surrounded by noisy children while sitting at the dining table with books and papers spread around him.

At this point I noticed that my energy and enjoyment of life were beginning to fade again. Those halcyon years of being depression-free were drawing to a close. In the summer of 1994, after four and half years of being well, I became aware of a gradual decline emotionally, physically and spiritually. By the autumn I was as ill as I had been before, and worse, for I went on to develop added complications.

Dad and Mum, with Roger and Sheila, 1944

Four girls, with Greta seated, in their grandparents' garden

The family on holiday, with Greta, front right

Greta, aged five, in her first school photo

Greta, 'always smiling', aged ten, at junior school,
back row, second from right

Greta and Adrian having fun with water and a bicycle pump

In 'sermons' dresses in garden

Part of a letter I wrote to Mum, telling her I loved her and would miss her, before one of my visits to the perpetrator's house

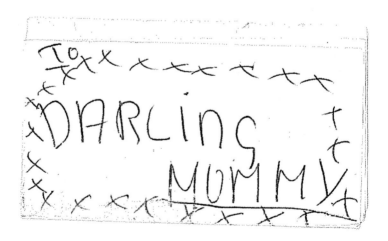

Marriage

of

Greta Pauline Cross

and

Ian Paul Randle

Saturday, April 10th, 1971
at 2 o'clock

10 April 1971 -
Greta's wedding day

The 'nice young man'

Greta

Greta and baby Nathan. 'I was sinking fast.'

Adam, Timothy and Nathan. 'The boys were my only joy.'

Ian and Greta, at Nathan's wedding

Ian, Mervyn, Greta and Lucy, out for lunch

Sheila, Zillah, Margaret and Greta, with Adrian behind, 'on the day I told them I was writing this book'

Greta, centre, meeting and greeting some of the women in
Chivatam village

Petals to welcome Ian and Greta at church in Nimmalagudem

6 'I don't love you any more'

I cried every day. Some days I just couldn't pull myself together and would lurch from one sobbing session to another. On other days I would take myself into the bathroom, let the tears flow there and then come back to the family and muddle through as best I could.

And I was afraid. Although I had been deeply depressed before, there were some differences this time round. The children were older, and once they were all safely delivered to school I would usually walk the dog and return home absolutely exhausted. I hadn't a clue how to deal with the symptoms. Should I lie on the sofa? Should I get on with housework and try to disregard my feelings? Turmoil became my constant companion: 'What should I do? If I give in and lie down, then what about tomorrow? I may want to lie down again, and what about the next day and the next and the next?'

Initially I dragged myself around the house doing what little I could. I would clear shower towels and pyjamas, bowls and cups and the general mayhem of a family breakfast. Each day there was washing and ironing and beds, and then the evening meal to prepare. It was a huge mountain to climb every morning, but I forced myself to do it all because

I feared resting. 'If I lie down today I might never be able to get back up again.'

My old confusion arose. I hadn't found any answer to it the first time round so my mind regurgitated it again: 'I am a Christian and I shouldn't be depressed.'

And the depression did not come alone this second time. It was punctuated by very severe migraines. Each one lasted between three and four days, following which I was totally washed out for another day. My body was forcing me to stop – in the end I had no choice but to rest.

At its worst the migraine gave me approximately seven or eight days' break before I was floored by another one. At best I was sometimes free of the pain for three weeks. The throbbing was desperately distressing. I cried as it thumped on my temple, but I hated crying because that only made things worse. It was a vicious cycle of crying in pain and the pain intensifying because of the crying. And as if that wasn't enough, a very dark creature took advantage of my weakness and vulnerability – dire despair.

It is hard to describe this despair because the feeling was so desperate; it was darker than dark, bringing with it a hopelessness that gripped me firmly. During the severest hours I lay in bed unable to lift my head without vomiting, often needing help to walk to the bathroom as the pain reverberated through my body and halted my steps. 'Is there ever going to be an end to this?' It seemed so hopeless. The answer seemed to bounce off the bedroom walls: 'No end, no light, no hope.' And so I would cry even more.

Well-meaning people would advise me about the dangers of chocolate and citrus fruit. I would buy the strongest over-the-counter analgesic tablets available. I would rub aloe gel on my aching forehead. I applied ice packs. I summoned Ian to hold my head and put pressure on the painful area. I began the search for the right prescription drugs, visiting the doctor many, many times. But nothing alleviated the agony.

The boys were concerned. Nathan would put his head around the bedroom door and ask, 'Are you OK, Mum?' He was frightened. I told him that I would be OK but right now I was not well.

In between these bouts my emotions were becoming more and more frayed. One morning I was trying to stop the tears. I thought to myself, 'I can't let Ian see me crying yet again.' I left the house with the dog. The route took me past the school that Timothy and Nathan were now attending. Walking by the school drive I had a feeling of complete emptiness. I began to think, 'If anything else happens to me now, I have no resources to cope. I am forty-two and I have no idea how I am going to live till I'm seventy.' I was at the end of my tether. I didn't know what to do next.

We continued until we reached an area where I could let Polly off her lead for a run. I wasn't thinking of anything or anyone in particular, just walking and keeping a watch on the dog. There was an old industrial area over the road which had become a demolition site. I glanced across at the mess, remembering our school speech days held in the conference hall that had previously been there. The dog chased backwards and forwards. At least one of us seemed happy.

I was glad to be out of the house. There was no-one else to consider and I didn't have to pretend that I was coping. I could just be myself and cry without feeling uncomfortable. But at times like these without distractions I was often faced with 'me'.

As I walked I saw a picture in my head of a small girl, curled around in a foetal position on an old battered sofa in the sitting room of the home where I had been born and lived until I had married. I didn't question who it was. I knew immediately it was me. Straight away I was certain about the cause of what was happening to me. I didn't know how it all connected together, but what I did know intuitively was that the abuse had come back to haunt me.

Now I really was confused. 'How on earth can that affect me now, after all these years?' I was absolutely convinced that I was right; the abuse was the root of the depression and all its debilitating symptoms, but the logic of it all evaded me. 'Surely that was then and this is now? How can that result in this?' My thoughts began to race round and round. I had always remembered what had happened to me, but year after year I had hardly ever thought about it. Sometimes I would think about a specific event but then I would push it to the back of my mind.

I was staggered and yet remained convinced that I was on the right track.

A short while after this I was listening to a programme on the radio regarding mental health and well-being. I was very interested as I could apply some of the things mentioned to my illness. At the end of the programme a telephone helpline was announced so I quickly jotted down the number. I did not hesitate at all. I needed information urgently. I phoned the number.

I didn't have to wait long before a female voice answered. I described the depression and, at risk of being shot down in flames, I said that I thought I was dealing with the sexual abuse of my childhood. But there weren't any flames. The next words I heard were so comforting and reassuring. The voice was kind and contained no criticism. This woman didn't think my theory derisory. Indeed she affirmed me by saying it was a serious possibility. After a very short conversation she recommended a book that she felt would be appropriate for me to read.

Books had always been a huge part of my life. I had always enjoyed reading. Mum had loved reading. As children we visited the local library, were given books as Sunday-school prizes and looked up information for homework in encyclopaedias. After we married, Ian and I accumulated hundreds of books, many of which were Bible study books, commentaries and other study aids.

Read a book? This woman was talking my language. It wasn't many days before I had acquired the book from the library and taken the first step of a very long journey of discovering just how my experiences as a child tied into my life as an adult.

Within the pages I found some of the exact things I had been feeling. It was strange. I would frequently experience something and then read about it. It wasn't that I read about the experience first and then somehow engineered that same thing. This comforted me because often it felt that my sanity was in danger of being destroyed. But these things had happened to others too – amazing.

The thirst for information increased. At the end of the first book I read through the bibliography to see what to read next. I did the same with each book I read. I went back to the library and, although I could find some of the books I wanted to read, I had to order others at the customer service desk. I was becoming a familiar face in the library.

Writing in my journal, which I had started in Yorkshire, had continued in fits and starts over the years but now I was scribbling in earnest. Although I was still depressed and lacking in energy, this stimulated me. Knowing there was help out there created an enthusiasm to search and understand the impact of the childhood me on the adult me. In some of the books there would be an end-of-chapter exercise or questions. My mind was telling me that if I read everything, answered all the questions and did the exercises I would soon be well. I just wanted to get it all over and done with and get back to normal. But, despite my enthusiasm for doing all these things, my illness and the discoveries I was making were taking their toll on my emotions and having a traumatic effect on our marriage.

I had started a new job and been at it long enough to begin getting bored with it, so I decided to look round for something more interesting. It was not long before I moved into working with older people in social services. I had had an idea that had first begun to develop when we were foster carers. We had met a number of different social workers in a variety of situations and the thought came to me that I could do that job myself. Getting a post with social services seemed a good step, but I didn't realise just how much it would help me progress with my career.

When I was established in the job the department sponsored me at the local college for a diploma course in welfare studies. It was interesting and I really enjoyed studying. However, I found the work, study, family and illness together far too big a load, but I couldn't stop. I drove myself harder and harder, prompted by an inner need to achieve, prove I could do it, and gain affirmation through the goals I constantly put in front of myself.

I was successful and the tutor encouraged me to apply to university for a social work course. Staff in the office told me horror stories of previous staff trying to get in but of not being successful despite several attempts. They were sure that my first attempt would be a good practice run but that I shouldn't pin my hopes on getting a place. I put together a portfolio of relevant work and studies, got invited for interview and was selected from seven hundred and fifty applicants to be one of fifty on the course. I was thrilled, but life was getting more and more difficult.

My job involved visits to elderly clients outside office hours to check that their carers were giving a good standard of service. One Sunday morning I had planned to visit a woman while her carer was with her. I needed to observe the carer at work and then chat with the client to see how she felt about our care service. But I never arrived. I felt agitated and restless. I didn't know what I wanted, but work was the last thing on my mind. I was at an utter loss; I was breaking up.

I drove across town towards her address but, instead of turning into her road, I went round the roundabout and back the way I had come. I pulled into a lay-by and lost track of time. As I sat in the car I cried and cried. My anguish was indescribable. The pit I was in was getting deeper and darker. There was no hope and no future for me.

I had written to my friend Sue:

> I feel there are all these different people in me. There's the one who is all in pieces inside, there's the professional at work, then there's the one who appears OK in public pushing the pram, doing the shopping, etc. There's another at church. A couple of people who know a little have expectations of me and others who know nothing have different expectations. Often with all these roles I have to put on a performance when what I really want is to be alone, do nothing and sleep.

I was continually running on empty and I was completely worn out. I felt that I had been carrying a heavy load of responsibility for the whole of my life. When I was a child I was responsible for carrying on as normal, responsible for the friendship between Velma and Mum, responsible for Roy's sexual gratification. And I had responsibility for the sexual knowledge that should not have been mine at such a young age. I had been made responsible and now I was exhausted by it all.

The support that I had got from Ian when I was first depressed was inconsistent the second time the illness reared its ugly head. He was completing his studies, exams were imminent, and at the bottom of his heart this course was not really what he wanted. At the time he had begun studying we had both felt there was no other option open to him, so he had enrolled. And so having made the commitment he threw himself into it and diligently worked to gain his qualifications. But spiritually and emotionally he was struggling.

The care and support that was such a part of what I offered to Ian over the years had dried up completely. He struggled with that. We rarely spoke about the things I was trying to sort out in my head. Like me, Ian was confused by it all but also felt let down that I was not able to support him to the level that he had become used to. Indeed, we were both feeling let down. This was a downward spiral of disappointment with each other and a feeling that we had each been failed.

In the summer of his final year at university Ian had to complete a work placement of several weeks. It was very difficult to get a placement at all, and one near home was not possible. So he was allocated to a probation department in a town about seventy miles away. It seemed that the only way to make this work was for Ian to stay locally to do his placement and return home at weekends.

Our relationship was rocky. We had tried to talk about things but we were continually misunderstanding each other and it felt as if we were hitting a brick wall. The idea of Ian being away from home seemed a good solution to me. He found a bed-and-breakfast place and went off on his placement early on Monday mornings, returning home on Thursday nights having worked four long days in order to get Fridays off.

We both looked forward to Mondays but dreaded Thursdays. Being apart suited us both. We each considered it better than the alternative of silent hostility or arguments. We had a little respite during the weekdays but weekends were often difficult.

My body was still struggling big time with the migraines and now I developed irritable bowel syndrome again. I had had it as a child but it had settled down after a while. When the pain came back in adulthood I recognised it at once.

I went for treatment but also talked to the doctor about emotional triggers. My hunch was right. My emotions were playing havoc with my physical frame.

But I had to press on. I was continually driven. In the summer of 1995 when Ian finished university and was applying for jobs, I was preparing to leave my job and start university.

The start of term arrived and the boys and I were all getting ready together. But my first two weeks at university were horrendous. I did OK in all the practical aspects of finding the right rooms on the campus and making myself known to a small group sitting near me, but emotionally I was falling apart. I was physically present in the lectures but hardly able to hold myself together. I had to go off to the toilets to cry in private and then present myself back in the room as if all was well. I had no idea why I was so overwhelmed.

But it became more manageable as time went on. I slipped into a routine of attending lectures and spending time in the library. At home I would get up early in the morning and put in a couple of hours of study before the boys needed to get ready for school.

But spiritually I was not able to do the things I had done for many years. My early-morning Bible readings were non-existent and I had no interest in talking to God because I thought he had no interest in me. After all, why was I in such a desperate place? Why was he not prepared to do a miracle and get me out of this mess? Why didn't he help Ian and me rather than watching us from a distance? Why was our previously happy marriage now floundering? God seemed totally uninterested in our plight.

During the twenty-four and a half years we had been married we had never owned a television. Our boys had been brought up on a diet of stories, games, music, outings, play areas, cycling, swimming and as many interests as we could fill their time with. But I came to a point where I wanted one. My mental distress was such that I felt there was no other escape from the thoughts and anguish constantly agitating my mind.

My enjoyment of reading had left me: I had no interest in books, apart from those I had to study. I had been able to bury myself in a book, but now I could no longer stay with a story long enough to get immersed in the plot. I thought that if I could just sit and stare at something for an hour it would ease things so that I could cope with the following hour. A television was the answer.

Christmas was getting near and my uncle gave us his television when he heard of our decision. He was getting a bigger and better version, and we even bought a video recorder to go with ours. It gave my mind a rest for short periods. I would become engrossed in a programme, and for that period of time all I thought of was what I was seeing on the screen. It was such a relief, although only temporarily.

One evening I was watching the news and there was an item about a woman who had been sexually abused as a child by her father. He had been convicted and imprisoned. Immediately I thought, 'So it's not too late then.' A seed had been sown. I thought about it a lot. I was convinced that the trauma I was experiencing now stemmed from that inflicted on me as a child. I tried to weigh it up in the light of my faith and I vacillated between 'Do I or don't I?' It wasn't long before I came to a definite decision.

Ian and I had heard about a seminar in a nearby town which was being presented by The Churches' Child Protection Advisory Service. It included information and statistics about abuse, church policy and a host of other things. I had spoken with Ian about what I had decided I was going to do, and after the seminar I approached one of the speakers. I had already decided that I was going to the police. The seminar speakers had confirmed it for me. Their words rang in my ears: 'It is a criminal offence. Use the proper authorities.'

We drove home in silence and then Ian said, 'Greta, you must do what you think is right.' I didn't need his 'permission' but it was good to hear this because it seemed to indicate that he was supportive. But when it actually came down to it the reality was that I was left to face my ordeal without him.

We were fast approaching our silver wedding anniversary. Over the years as a family we had enjoyed holidays on canal boats. We loved being outside and seeing towns and the country from a different perspective. We all enjoyed having a go at manning the tiller. Even the dog was in her element with so much freedom to run along the canal banks as often as she wanted. It was great fun. Ian and I had made a plan some time previously: for our silver wedding anniversary we would hire a luxury boat for the two of us. We had looked forward to it for a long time. However, by the time the anniversary came round, our relationship seemed in no state to give rise to celebration.

But we went. It was a magnificent area of hilly country which gave us some picturesque views from the level of the canal. We stopped at a quaint town where we went to the cinema and then to church the next morning. We negotiated locks, and I walked along the path with the dog while Ian gently steered the boat alongside us. But then the day of our anniversary dawned.

We gave each other a gift but the celebrations were very muted. I had intimated to Ian that I would like a flute as I thought it was a fitting silver gift. But I had noticed that nothing vaguely flute-shaped had been packed when we had set off. I gave him the benefit of the doubt however and waited until the day. But it didn't materialise. I was angry: this was the final straw in an already strained relationship. I made sure he knew that after twenty-five years I didn't think it was too much to ask for something special. Ian said that he felt we had spent a considerable amount on the hire of the boat and he regarded *that* as the celebration. So the day went downhill and the tension between us mounted.

That evening we located a canal-side pub. We made our selection from the menu and ordered drinks. But we sat in silence during the whole of the meal. I looked across at another couple huddled together in a corner having a very animated conversation. As they talked they touched and stroked each other. While they were eating they would offer each other food from their forks. They were a picture of happiness.

As I watched it seemed to exacerbate the chasm that was developing between Ian and me. I thought to myself, 'I have been married to this man for twenty-five years but I can't think of a word to say to him.' My mouth felt dry and the food seemed like sawdust, but somehow we ate our meal. We left the pub as soon as possible.

On arriving back at the boat Ian unlocked it and walked off down the canal path. I watched him go and inside I began to panic. Although our relationship was at an all-time low, we had been so dependent on each other that being without him was a painful thought. I needed him so that I had someone who needed me! It was a very distorted premise to build any relationship on, but now even that was crumbling. I wondered where he was going and what he would do. Would he ever come back?

Eventually Ian came back to the boat and without any explanation from him we went quietly to bed.

The next morning was equally quiet. We were both on automatic pilot, showering, breakfasting, attending to the dog and sorting the weed hatch in the stern. We got the jobs done and then sat down together. Ian asked very sadly, 'What's gone wrong with us?' I looked across at him and thought about the last few years. We had tried to talk about things, but it felt to me that I was on one side of the fence and he was on the other, and I was also piggy-in-the-middle trying to explain to him what it was like to be me. We were unable to find a way of making progress. He just didn't understand what was happening and, unlike me with my strategy of searching out information, Ian used a different way of coping. He buried himself in his own pain and hoped mine would somehow get better and we would be back to how we had been.

I was aware of the motion of the canal under us and I heard ducks tapping on the side of the boat, but we both remained quiet, lost in our own thoughts. I knew I had to say it, knew I couldn't go on pretending any longer, though I also knew it would send him even further down than he already was, but I replied, 'I will never leave you because of the boys but I don't love you any more.'

7 'It's a figment of her imagination'

Having made up my mind that the abuse should be reported to the police, I wanted to speak to my sisters. There were things I partially remembered and other pieces of the jigsaw that needed fitting into my picture. They had no idea of the emotional journey I had started on. I asked them if we could all meet together. This meeting didn't include Adrian because I didn't think there had been any criminal actions involving him. But when he learned what was happening he offered his full support and reassured us that he was there if we needed him.

By this time I had been in the second period of depression for over a year. It was November 1995 and we met in Zillah's home. I shied away from using our house because I was uncertain of what Ian's response would be. I was beginning to feel there were vibes of disapproval coming from him, and I didn't feel I could talk to him at length about any of the things I was feeling.

When we were all together we chatted for a while and then I took 'the chair'. I started by telling them about how I had been depressed. This was quite difficult in itself. The four of us were strong, capable, competent women in many ways. Zillah and I in particular often shrugged things off, had little regard for analysing cause and effect, and just 'got on' with our lives. Some weeks before the meeting I had spoken tentatively with Zillah about being 'a bit fed-up'. She asked me what it was about and I broached the subject of the childhood sexual abuse. She expressed surprise but didn't reject my idea out of hand. But now I was trying again to relate the little I understood to more of my siblings.

There were disjointed events in my head that I had sometimes thought about, and I wanted the family to hear them and fill in any gaps that they remembered.

'Do you remember one Sunday night after church when our family were all asked to stay behind while Velma had her say? What was that all about?' I asked. Each one who could recall the incident offered me a little more information.

'And what about when Mum and Sheila went off into the front room and talked together?' Then someone mentioned that there had been an offhand remark by Velma when we were all still very young: 'It's just a figment of her imagination.' The temperature rose and we each got very animated. There was indignation and some anger as we pieced together snippets of conversations from years ago.

But as we exorcised some of our hidden feelings within the safety of Zillah's home we became quieter and more thoughtful. In my heart I knew the next step I was going to take whether anyone else took it with me or not. We each sat with our own thoughts for a few minutes and then I broke the silence. 'What do we do next?' I had hardly paused for breath when Margaret spoke: 'We're going to the police.' I had one ally at least. Zillah spoke next and said she was right behind us, but Sheila voiced some hesitation. I considered that three out of four was more than sufficient, and I was happy to have just the three bringing a case, so I said to her, 'It's OK; don't feel you have to go along with us. We'll do it, but it will be for you as well.' We agreed together that we would do the reporting by telling our own stories, but Sheila was giving it more thought. After a minute or two she decided she would join us. We fixed a date to go as a group to the police station.

That afternoon together was both helpful and unhelpful to me. My sisters had been able to help me piece together a fuller picture of things by adding their memories to mine. But there had been something else niggling in my mind which I had been compelled to ask them.

During the previous few months I had been plagued by the worry that perhaps Mum had known what had been happening to me. But I was a mum now and knew just how much I loved my children and how much I would give to protect them from being hurt. Surely if she'd known she would have stuck up for me, would have gone round to Roy's house and said something, would have stopped me going there ever again? 'Surely you would have done that for me, Mum?'

I wrote a letter to her although I knew there was no-one to post it to and I had no hope of a reply. I sat on a bench near her grave and spoke out my questions from the page.

'Weren't there any tell-tale signs? I couldn't retaliate, could I, Mum, because I was brought up to be a good girl and not say "no" to adults? Why did you keep sending me there with no second thought? Why didn't you put a stop to it?' But the wind carried away my words. I knew she couldn't answer and I didn't really want to hear her answers anyway. If she had known during my childhood, how could I live with that knowledge?

But now I knew.

Because I hadn't been reading the Bible and following the systematic approach I usually took, when I picked it up after a break of many months I didn't know where to start. It seemed so aimless just to pick it up and start reading. But I needed some way of finding comfort, direction, answers, so on the odd occasion I would read a psalm. I considered that each one was able to stand alone without having to be read with masses of background information. I thought it might give me a straw at which I could grasp. But nothing helped.

Then I read from a psalm that was a picture of what was happening to me. It talked about darkness, being as low as possible in the deepest despair. The writer felt the same as me, for he too had wanted to die. There was a change of tone then as he called to God to help him out of his mess. Next there was action, telling how God stamped around heaven in readiness to mount a rescue, and it painted a picture of God coming down and lifting this man from the pit. He was in a desperate state of inner darkness but he wrote, 'You, LORD, keep my lamp burning.'[1]

I was deeply impressed. In spite of the fact that God and I were not on speaking terms, I was not listening to him and I didn't pray any more, he was still keeping my spirit alive.

It didn't feel to me that my spirit was alive but I chose to think about those words. I was convinced that my years of being a Christian were over. God did not seem to be around for me. I felt totally abandoned. But then the words would come back to me again: 'You, O LORD, keep my lamp burning.' If I was going to survive this then someone had to keep me going, because I knew *I* couldn't do it. But it seemed to me that on the occasions I remembered these words they helped a little.

The reading seemed to indicate that when God hears a small cry of help he can't wait to come to the rescue. Were my tears and crying a way of asking God to come and help me? Was he actually closer than I had given him credit for? Could he and I together cope with the confirmation I now had that Mum had known what had been going on.

* * *

81

University was going well. I enjoyed studying and there were one or two women who had joined with me to form a study group. I was making good academic progress, with respectable marks for my assignments. Some days were more manageable than others, but generally I continued to be despondent, tearful and fragile.

Within the student services that were available, counselling was on offer. The only thing I knew about counselling was from a module I had studied. And I had tried counselling a while before with a counsellor who was part of our doctor's practice. It was not a good experience. She seemed to be out of her depth and had no appreciation of the traumatic impact of childhood sexual abuse. I attended only twice and thought I was better off just continuing to read and write about things as they arose. But I began to ponder whether or not it might be an idea to ask for an appointment with a university counsellor. In the end I decided that I had nothing to lose. It couldn't be any worse than my other experience, and it might even be better.

But there was an initial hitch: I was appointed a male counsellor. That threw me a little, but I had no idea that I could have voiced my reservations and asked for a female. However, after two sessions he became ill and went off on long-term sick leave. That made me feel guilty. Here was I talking about myself when all the time he was ill. I was soon offered an appointment with another counsellor, but did I really want to talk to another person and tell my story all over again? I decided to try. I met with Jane and we began the counselling process for what was actually the third time.

Jane was amazing. She listened and understood. She led me gently through difficult emotions. She challenged me to give thought to how I might look after myself. And then we addressed the issue of reporting the abuse to the police. We explored this week by week. She made me aware of some of the things I had not thought about.

'What about the outcome: how will you feel if he is found not guilty? What if you don't feel the punishment fits the crime?' We talked about going to court and what the impact of it all might be. And of course I talked about Ian and how my problems were taking their toll on our marriage. The counselling continued for many months.

After meeting together as siblings and actually going to the police I did something amazingly foolish. While preparing to report the abuse, I had written to the last-known address I had for Roy. I knew that since Velma's death he had remarried and moved house. However what I didn't know was that he still owned the old house and occasionally went back and picked up his post. I thought that I would need his new address to give to the police. Of course on one level I knew that the police find people and addresses, but I felt that if I was going to do this properly I wanted as much information as I could lay my hands on.

While I was out one day Roy phoned our home in response to the card I had sent. Fortunately I didn't have to speak to him, but he gave Ian his new address and a phone number, never suspecting what was in store. But then something in me wanted to confront him. Confrontation was something I usually avoided, but I needed to take the bull by the horns and address the person who had controlled me for so many years.

It was almost ten o'clock one night and Ian had gone to work, the younger boys were in bed and Adam was out. I picked up the phone and dialled Roy's number. I was both relieved and scared when he rather than his wife picked up the phone. I told him who it was and he was surprised. But then I launched into my prepared speech: 'What you did to me years ago was a criminal offence. As a family we are currently considering what action to take.' He blurted out, 'I am sorry, I am so sorry, I am sorry.' I didn't want to hear it. Politely I said, 'Goodnight' and put down the phone.

I couldn't believe what I had done. I began to shake. But then I remembered that he had my phone number and might try to phone back. I snatched up the receiver again and phoned Zillah.

'You'll never guess what I've just done,' I said. I told her about the call and we chatted for about half an hour. If he was trying to phone he wouldn't be able to get through. But now that the conversation was over, the line was free again. The dreaded fear was back – Roy was still controlling me. Immediately I unplugged the phone and did what I often did when life was difficult: I went to bed and slept to try to obliterate him from my mind. That night was the last time I ever spoke to him.

Our plans to go to the police seemed to trigger even more deterioration between Ian and me. Throughout our marriage I had been the one who had offered support to him. After all, I had been a nurse with a caring disposition. I wanted to look after people and here was a golden opportunity: a husband who soaked up my tender loving care like a sponge. I gave time, support and encouragement, never once begrudging any of it. But things had changed and now I needed someone to take charge of things for me.

I had been falling apart for a number of months and crying excessively. The last thing I could think about was being there for someone else. I wasn't able to give to Ian any longer but neither could Ian give me what I needed. I resented that. I began brick by brick to build a wall between us. And now, as well as studying at university, I was also starting a process that would have a traumatic impact.

One day we four sisters turned up together at the police station and told the duty officer at the front desk that we wished to report several instances of historic child abuse. He looked from one to the other of us and said he would contact a colleague to take us through to a room where we could sit and talk. We didn't have to wait long before a young woman police officer arrived. This was the start of almost a year of police visits, telephone calls, court appearances – and a verdict.

After just a couple of weeks the same female officer came to our home to interview me. I had planned an afternoon appointment so that we could talk freely while the boys were at school. She had said it would probably take two hours to take my statement. We chatted in the kitchen while I made coffee and then settled down to the business in hand.

'Can you tell me about the occasions when you were abused?' I had to give precise and clinical details. I described rooms and events, recalled words spoken to me and gave as much information as I could. I was asked questions to clarify events in as much detail as possible:

'Were there any lights on?' and 'Did he say anything to you?' and 'Did he ever give you presents or money?' There were many more questions. I gave as much information as my memory would allow. It was unemotional and without a tear. I appeared cold and in control. So the first interview was over. I had done it. It was all out in the open. Now someone other than my family knew.

The police took statements from us all separately in our own homes. After all the interviews were complete they phoned to tell us that they would be making a dawn call on Roy's house to arrest him. Following the arrest they told us he was in custody being interviewed.

I was terribly anxious. I felt like a naughty child who had done something that the adults didn't like. 'What will his wife think of all this? What will Ann think of me? What will our old friends in his denomination think?' I hated the thought that I would not be liked or that people would think badly of me. I had always been liked as a child and teenager because I was compliant, did what the adults wanted me to do and never made any waves. But now I was moving out of my compliance zone and headlong into facing my adversary.

January 1996 saw the start of the case at the local magistrates' court. At his arrest Roy had admitted most of the offences and was putting in a guilty plea. This meant that he would not be tried by a jury and we would not be called to give evidence. It was a huge relief. However we agreed that we would attend.

Ian was not at work early so he was around while the boys were getting ready for school. I was not going to university that day although it was a normal day for lectures, but I hadn't told Ian. He looked at the clock and commented, 'Have you seen the time? You need to get going.' I was in the pantry getting things together for the boys' lunch boxes.

'I'm not going today, it's the court date,' I said. Ian's retort was immediate and sharp: 'It's not worth missing a day at university for that; it will only be deferred.' That did it! We said no more. I was in tears. I slammed the pantry door, banged around the kitchen getting the lunches made and walked out of the house.

Throwing my bag into the car, I drove to university. I was angry, driving aggressively and fast. I flew down the motorway but justified it to myself by thinking that it would make up a bit of lost time. My thoughts were in a complete scramble but I remembered the 'trust' game we had played as children. Two people would stand one behind the other. The one in front would fall back and trust the person behind to catch them. As children we caught each other because we realised that the consequences of letting someone fall on their back, crashing on the floor, could be serious. Before actually taking the plunge and falling though, we would turn our head and check to see that the other person was waiting and prepared.

It seemed to me that the morning's incident was serious for Ian and me. After many years of catching him and picking him up from some of his bad times, I needed reciprocation. And just when I needed him to say something like, 'Will you be OK at court? Would you like me to come?' it seemed I had turned round in my desperation and there was no-one there to catch me. I felt distraught.

In the weeks leading up to the court date I had been thinking about how I would feel when Roy was in the same room. I wondered if we would have to see each other in the waiting area. I thought about whether or not the family would be with him. How would I handle it? The last straw broke the camel's back. Ian didn't seem to appreciate the magnitude of what was happening. The person I should have been closest to was now a million miles away.

8 'Take him down!'

At lunch break on the day of the court case I phoned one of my sisters to ask what had gone on during the morning. She was livid. I quietly asked her what had happened but she was so angry with me.

'Where were you?' she shouted down the phone.

'Ian and I had a row and I came over to my lectures,' I replied.

'You did what? We were all waiting for you. Why didn't you come?' She was not letting me off lightly. I had been the one who had told my family how deeply affected I had been. I had called the meeting to set the ball in motion. And now I was the one who hadn't put in an appearance on the first day of this important process.

She told me that it had been adjourned to a further date a few weeks away at the magistrates' court. Roy had simply confirmed his name and offered a guilty plea, and another date had been set.

There were lots of things I wanted to ask but Zillah was in such a rage that I just said we would talk later. What did he look like? Who was with him? Did you have to sit near him? Were his family upset? Did they want to speak to you? How did you all cope? Were you all OK? There was so much to find out. I felt guilty: I had let them down and I felt severely chastened. I went back to lectures and waited, but with little interest in what I was hearing.

I no longer loved Ian but we were hanging in there, still under the same roof, offering little to each other but working together for the sake of the boys. However, the first day of the court case seemed to me like the final nail in the coffin of our marriage. There seemed no hope of being able to bridge the gap.

While studying I had come across an article about the partners of child sexual abuse survivors. It talked about what they needed in a relationship. The writer described how the demands of a survivor upon the partner can mean that the future prospects for the relationship are poor. Our marriage seemed to be in that category: poor. I knew that I would never end our marriage but I felt that it was impossible to improve it. Things had gone too far.

Over the years we had frequently been to Spring Harvest, a large Christian event on the Butlin's site in Skegness. I was often the driving force behind this because it was something I enjoyed, and the boys too were keen to go. There were age-appropriate activities each morning and evening, and during the afternoons we would accompany them swimming or find ourselves watching interminable fairground rides. As they grew older they had a lot of freedom to stay out late, attending concerts and late-night chat shows and generally having a good time.

One year I had an experience that gave me a glimmer of hope. In the 'big top' one evening there was an opportunity for people to explore different ways of meeting together in worship. In an area to the side of the main congregation there were large boards on which people were painting while the rest of the service carried on. I felt inspired to go and try my hand at some art. It was never one of my best skills, and some of the work was obviously being done by very talented people: big and bold, colourful and vibrant, powerful and moving. I waited until there was no-one else around, and I walked down and picked up a paintbrush. My offering was tiny. When I approached the board I had no idea what was about to come from the end of the brush. I painted a very small urn. It was black. Then, using several colours, I flicked the brush across the page to form arcs coming out of the pot. I felt that God used this to speak to me: 'From the blackness of your experience, I will bring colour back to your life, which will spread out and reach others.'

But there were a couple of years at Spring Harvest when Ian and I had argued and been unable to resolve our differences. Ian remonstrated emphatically, 'We're not coming here again.' Sometimes there were many tears and frustrations as we were both in our own different worlds, wanting the other to appreciate our individual difficulties. But it was impossible. We were so distressed that there was no way we could walk even a step in the other's shoes, let alone a mile!

But the next year we were back at Skegness. We were in the big top one night and things that were said from the platform resonated with how Ian and I were feeling. We turned to each other and decided that it might be a good idea to go forward for prayer.

On the platform we had noticed a man, John, whom we had known since we were teenagers. We knew he had gone on to become a minister and had been very successful. There had been no close contact over the years, but we had seen each other and chatted occasionally. We wondered whether, as he knew us, he would come and pray with us.

'How about asking John if he has some time tomorrow to meet for coffee and a chat?' I asked. Ian was open to this idea and we were able to approach John as he was leaving the platform. He was heavily committed to seminars and other things but said he had an hour in the afternoon when we could meet up.

So the following day we met John. We told him a little of what had been happening, describing the depression, the disarray in our marriage and the underlying sexual abuse. John knew the perpetrator from the meetings and youth events we had attended together as young people. As he expressed his shock and horror, he said something to Ian that felt so supportive for me: 'If it had been my wife, Ian, I would have gone and punched him!'

I wanted to leap up waving my arms in the air shouting, 'Go for it!' Instead I turned to see Ian's reaction. Here was another Christian, our age, with similar theological understanding to us and similar values, and he wanted to punch someone! This was not the Christianity we knew. This was not a part of the nice Christian values with which we had been indoctrinated. This was not acceptable behaviour. But I was ecstatic. Here was someone being real and human. This was what I was looking for – someone to be on my side, to protect me, to look after me. That was what I wanted from Ian.

Ian was shocked. But he had some food for thought. There was another conversation to be had when we could get some time together. But there was a shock for me too. Ian told John about how he was feeling. He had had difficulties of his own with redundancy and going down a completely different career path from the one he had imagined. And it was all compounded by trying to process what was happening to me and our marriage. I began to think about how I had been so wrapped up in my own journey that I had built a wall between us. I had become bitter and unloving, and now Ian was telling John something that smashed through my selfish thoughts. I heard him say, 'I don't want to live any longer.'

I was stunned. I had no idea that Ian had reached this point. We hadn't been able to talk at this depth. Each of us was so damaged and hurting that it had prevented us from supporting and helping the other. In my head I was asking, 'Where do we go from here?'

For a few weeks things were better between us, but we didn't talk about the issues that really needed our attention. I was afraid because I had been down that route too many times and all it led to was yet another misunderstanding and more frustration. From the outside it looked better, but on the inside we were both hurting and had no idea how to get to the heart of our problems.

In our earlier years of marriage we had been proud of the fact that we had been able to communicate. We had always talked together about things and come to a resolution fairly easily. We had loved each other and worked things through. These were some of the values on which we based our relationship. But the dire change in me and the confusion of it all in both our minds meant that the way we had usually done things was just not working now. We were in too deep.

On the one hand I was trying to resolve marriage difficulties and parent our children, but then there were other times when I felt that *I* was the child.

For many years we had travelled to the Isle of Wight each summer. Ian and I did voluntary work at a children's camp and of course the boys had a really good holiday joining in all the activities.

One afternoon the children were all off-site with group leaders. Some were horse riding, others had gone to a theme park and another group were on the beach. Ian and I went out together for a couple of hours and found ourselves in Godshill. The camp was hard work but we knew it was worthwhile. The children were all from deprived areas and our aim was to give them a very good holiday away from their poor and difficult backgrounds.

We were so tired that we sat in the garden of a tea room making our cream scones last as long as possible. But then we mustered enough energy to have a walk around the village and look in the shops.

In one particular shop window I saw a golly. It was years since I had seen one and it was very reasonably priced. I wanted it. I really wanted it.

'I would love that golly,' I said to Ian. But we went on and continued our circuit of the small streets. I didn't know why I wanted the golly or why I wanted it so much. I mentioned it again. At the end of our walk, we went back to the shop and Ian bought it for me. At the end of camp Golly came home and sat in our bedroom.

One afternoon in winter Timothy needed a lift to the cinema, but Nathan came up with an idea for himself. Timothy and his friend could go to their film and he would go to see *Matilda* on another screen. Nathan was a very keen reader and had read quite a few Roald Dahl books, so seeing the film was quite a reasonable request.

But I did not want to go. Logically I could see why it would work well, with each boy seeing what he wanted, but I lay on the sofa quietly crying because I didn't want to go. I had a tantrum and threw a book across the room, but then I said, 'OK, I'll take you.'

It was already dark, and as I drove to the cinema tears were streaming down my face because I was being forced into doing something I didn't want to do. Nathan and I went into our showing of *Matilda* and I continued to cry. I was so distressed but couldn't pull myself out of it. The strength of feeling was overwhelming and I was glad to get home to where I felt safe again. The boys went to bed and I wrote about it in my journal.

I knew that this type of thing was not an isolated incident; it was somehow connected to other things. I found another book that helped me understand why I was acting so child-ishly. More work, more questions to answer and more exercises at the end of each chapter.

My emotions were sometimes inappropriate too. One day Zillah and I had been out with the dogs. She had always been fond of animals and we would often go together to exercise both her dog and mine. We were making our way from the fields back to the car when something she said made me laugh. But my emotions were in a tangle, and in a strange way although I wanted to laugh it never came out that way, so instead I began to cry. Everything was so near the surface that I didn't feel safe expressing myself because it was becoming so embarrassing.

Then the court date came round again. The magistrate had sent the case to the crown court several miles away in our county town. I had attended the second appearance before the magistrate, but since then reports had been prepared, barristers appointed and the four of us had turned up for early meetings with different people at the crown court.

It was at the magistrates' court that I had come face to face with Roy. I was standing in the lobby area and his family were gathered together with another person whom I recognised. I was deeply uncomfortable. I didn't want to make any eye contact so I made sure I wasn't looking in their direction. I felt that they were condemning me. And then to my right a door opened and out walked Roy. I was in the wrong place at the wrong time. He stepped forward and I froze to the spot. I wanted to turn round and run out but my feet were pinned to the floor by fear. We looked at each other but he didn't stop. He walked right in front of me and across to his family and friend on the opposite side.

That memory lingered and was all too vivid in my mind as I faced the crown court appearance. I was still worried about what others thought of me and what his family were going through. I remained terrified of being in his presence. But I also knew that what I was doing was right.

A representative from Victim Support greeted us and gave us an insight into the proceedings and the courtroom. He told us where everyone would be sitting and what to expect. He had agreed with the judge that we could sit together in the jury seats as there was no jury. This meant that we would not be seated in the main public area with Roy's family.

And then he took us into the dock. I was petrified! Things were upside down in my head. I was blaming myself for what was happening. I had second thoughts about the wisdom of it all and on top of that I would be seeing my abuser. Silent tears began to roll down my cheeks. One by one my sisters noticed and offered tissues, a hand, a hug, and then we stepped down.

Next we met our barrister. We were ushered into an intricately arranged screened-off area in the very large foyer of the court building. The large hall was extremely old, ornate and echoing. Shoes tapped across the tiles; voices of small groups of people reverberated. Court ushers were directing and calling for people. Behind the screens it seemed hushed as we all huddled together. Our barrister went through some of the things he would be saying, and assured us that it would be fairly straightforward as Roy had already pleaded guilty. He was warm and friendly but also had the efficient air of the professional getting on with his job. He expressed his sympathy with our situation but then left quite hastily, black gown flapping in his wake.

We stayed there for a few minutes and then proceeded into the foyer ready to go into court. Roy and his family were as far away as it was possible to be from our group as we all lingered waiting to be taken into the courtroom.

It wasn't long before we were called through to take our seats. A catalogue of offences was read out and the plea was noted: guilty. The defence and the prosecution presented their findings. I was incensed by the defence barrister as he labelled the offences 'antiquated'. I was further enraged as he protested that the perpetrator had suffered by 'having to face his family and tell the church'. He described how Roy 'was not a robust man' and 'had poor health'. And then to add insult to injury we were called 'precocious children'!

I was boiling inside but unable to say a word to my sisters as I wanted to keep up with all that was going on. Our barrister balanced things by speaking of the impact on our lives and marriages, and the far-reaching effects of childhood trauma on the victims. Moreover he said that 'if ever there was a case that proved the long-lasting effects of the abuse of young children, this is it'.

The judge summed up by talking of the gravity of such a case involving innocent children. He spoke directly to Roy, stating: 'You were in a position of trust and the offences continued over a long period of time. They were committed against young, defenceless girls and have had an ongoing adverse effect on those girls, now women, over a substantial period of their lives.'

Anxiously we awaited his decision. Finally he was drawing to a close and soon we would know the outcome. And then the judge pronounced his verdict: 'I have no option but to give you a custodial sentence . . . Take him down.'

9 'No sex, please, we're British'

Many times Ian and I would start a conversation with the best of intentions. We were still together and occasionally trying to have another go at talking things through. It was discouraging because more often than not nothing was resolved and, after our conversations, rather than being better, our relationship was worse. There seemed to be a bigger rift and a higher wall between us than ever.

On one occasion we were in our bedroom, getting increasingly agitated. I was desperate to make Ian understand my feelings but he wanted me to understand his. We were walking a tightrope from two opposite ends but somehow we never met in the middle. We couldn't agree and neither could we compromise, so we were stuck. In my anger I shouted at Ian, 'When we married you promised "for better, for worse". You've had the best and now it's the worst.'

These struggles were clearly evident in our sexual relationship. When we first got married it took time to settle into being together and living the 24/7 relationship after a traditional courtship. However, the constraints of singleness and no sex outside marriage were gone. We were now a legal couple and made the most of it.

Occasionally I would point out things that were uncomfortable for me. When we were in the kitchen Ian would sometimes stand close behind me and put his arms around me. I didn't like it and would snap, 'Stop it.' At other times, if he approached quietly I would jump out of my skin with an extremely startled reaction and shout, 'Don't do that!' I didn't realise why these things were upsetting, so I would fly off the handle and then return quickly, apologise and be back to normal.

But we were young and having fun and most of the time it was exciting just to be together and explore our sexuality.

On other occasions getting more intimately close gave me flashbacks. As we began to make love my mind was often haunted by a picture of a large pair of hands, as if they were right in front of my face. I hated those hands. Just under my breath I would keep saying, 'It's OK; it's Ian, not Roy.' I repeated it several times, trying to convince myself that what was happening would be good. Sometimes I was successful, other times not. My thinking was, 'Just get through this in one piece and of course the next time will be fine.'

After the 'newly married' stage we managed for a number of years. I compromised a lot and was often unhappy about the demands made on me. But generally I was able to give sufficient to appease. However I never instigated any sexual activity and was often a reluctant participant. It was far from ideal but I made up for it in other ways. After all, I looked after the children, supported Ian in his work, baked, entertained and kept the house spick and span in addition to my part-time work.

But there was one isolated week when things were different. Ian was away at a children's camp but I stayed back with Nathan. I really missed Ian and looked forward to joining him for the second week, as we had planned.

We had done camp work together for a number of years and knew it was demanding, and that year was no different. We worked hard, and within the canvas of our tent we played hard too. I was the instigator and I had a willing respondent. But that was short-lived. It was just one week of a glimpse into what could have been. And when our relationship deteriorated the sex deteriorated even further too.

No Sex, Please, We're British was a long-running London West End comedy for about sixteen years from 1971, the year we married. We began to use that phrase initially as a bit of a joke, but as time went on it was no longer a joke, and certainly there was no comedy being played out in our house. It was all very grave and serious.

I tried. I knew it was part of marriage. I knew it was unfair to Ian that I had been damaged by crimes that had nothing to do with him. I knew he had needs and desires that were perfectly valid. I was flattered because he wanted me and found me attractive, but I was unable to respond. Initially I would refuse, then I would feel guilty and give in, but afterwards I would feel abused all over again. It was a dreadful cycle and we would lie together with both of us in tears, apologising to each other, both depressed by the mess we were in.

Some of those times were so distressing that I was completely beside myself. I was racked with deep sobs and anger that what had been done to me was making me into this unresponsive, asexual being. I would cry and cry, hurting so much, and completely overwhelmed by the despair. I would try to explain to Ian how much I hated what I had been made into, but I could hardly speak, catching my breath, with my body shaking. Inside I was thinking that this would never end, never stop hurting. I would never be normal. I was furious. Those times left me exhausted. Over the following twenty-four hours I would be almost silent and just get on with things quietly. But in a strange way, although the issue came between us, it also brought us closer. It was not just my pain. We were both directly affected by the abuse. But we didn't know how to heal the deep woundedness we both felt.

10 'How will I know when it's all gone?'

Counselling was a very private space purely for me. While at university I looked forward to every meeting with Jane. Talking about myself was a completely new concept. My life had shaped me to be a listener. I was the one who often encouraged other people to talk. Being asked to talk was amazing.

I once wrote in my journal, 'This week I have felt invisible. Who am I? Am I a person at all? It just seems no-one wants to listen to me. I feel so unimportant. Who is interested? Who wants to know about me, my pain, my feelings?'

As a child I had never been asked to express an opinion or invited to contribute to conversations. I was not allowed to challenge or disagree with anyone. I wasn't encouraged to develop social skills. I picked some up along the way, but my development was more by luck than good judgment. The abuse compounded my lack of social skills. It seemed that not being able to talk naturally to adults about anything had kept me from talking at a deep level about what was happening to me.

As a teenager and young adult I had no confidence that people would want to listen to me, so I avoided expressing much about myself. I would keep to safe topics, not speaking about anything controversial because I hated conflict, and it was all due to having experienced a major family upset.

When I was about eight or nine I had come home from school one day during the long, warm summer to find that Adrian had not arrived. At that time he and I were in two separate buildings of the same school, with separate playgrounds, and the two different age groups didn't mix at all. I was a junior and he was an infant.

This was not the first time he had been late home. We knew the drill. Our parents would send each of the four girls out to look for him. Mum would stay at home so that someone would be there if he turned up. We had done this several times before. We set off towards all points of the compass: one up the road, another one round to a parallel road and another to the recreation ground. Often when we had trekked round our particular route we would return home within minutes of one another and, lo and behold, we would find that our little brother had returned. All was well.

However, on this occasion he was still not back by the time Dad came home from work at around five o'clock. We had been sent out again and this time a little further afield. While I was out I felt a dreadful sinking anxiety and hoped desperately that when I got back Adrian would be there.

We forgot all about tea that night. No-one ate, but we didn't seem to notice either. I have no idea who decided to act, but at some stage my parents informed the police of Adrian's absence. Tension mounted and the levels of anxiety in the family became almost palpable.

It was around nine in the evening when the police arrived. They had found Adrian and his friend Baghi Singh in the old air-raid shelters under the town hall. Both were safe. Almost . . .

As soon as the police had gone, our relief was indescribable. But Mum felt such anger, mixed with the release of tension, that she flew violently at my brother, raining her fists down on him. Dad was horrified. This was his only son, his cherished boy. This was the son he had waited patiently for after the death of his firstborn son. He was having none of it. In his anger he flew at Mum. They raised their voices and flung fists at each other. Some of us were crying, and at this point I ran terrified through the door out into the yard. I stood there not knowing what to do. I just wanted it all to stop. I felt so ashamed. And I never spoke a word about it to anyone for the next thirty years.

My introduction to conflict and disagreement was not healthy. I internalised these events, and the resulting damage from that evening was that as an adult I was not able to conduct myself coherently in the presence of any sign of conflict for many years.

Apart from being amazed that the counsellor had asked me to speak about myself, I was a little cautious because this was new territory. But I relished it! A whole hour to tell another person anything I wanted to. But not just one hour, an hour week after week after week.

Initially I didn't know where to start. There was so much to tell. Things that had never been told. Things that were shameful. Things that were embarrassing. Things that hurt. So many things . . . and once I started, I could hardly stop.

My main support during a period of about eighteen months and especially during the court case had come from Jane. I had relied heavily on her as the proceedings started. I had talked at length about my feelings about having to see Roy in court. I knew that if he or his family spoke to me or challenged me I would want to run. I was very frightened but I was able to express it all within the counselling room. I had also spoken with her about the deep feelings of wanting to opt out of any more turmoil and pain by dying.

Jane had a holiday coming up. Yet she knew how vulner-able I was. I was anxious about the three-week period in which I would not be able to see her. So she outlined a plan. I would write in my diary for an hour during each of those weeks while she was away. I would spend each of those hours in a quiet place on my own writing down the things I wanted to talk to her about. She wanted me to record how I was feeling, what was happening and how I was coping. She talked me through some DIY counselling as a strategy for her absence. It was a short-term solution, and soon she was back and we were able to pick up where we had left off.

My fellow students had no idea what was happening. Ian and I didn't talk to each other about our individual experiences and feelings so, although he knew that I was being counselled, we never discussed what went on. Sometimes I would talk with my sisters but that was mostly about things to do with the court case and our feelings about that. Occasionally I would describe myself as being 'a bit fed up' but I never talked in depth about being depressed and the impact it was having.

During my three years at university there were two occasions when I seriously considered throwing in the towel. I had always lived life with as many activities as I could fit in, assuming that everyone juggled as many things as I did.

But when it all caught up with me I doubted my ability to achieve my goal. I had the option of doing two years of study and gaining a diploma in social work, but from the start this had never been my intention. I wanted to do more. I wanted to do a third year and get not only the diploma but also a degree. Moreover I also wanted to get an honours degree, so during the final year I needed to do a research project and write a dissertation.

I had to consider what to do. I would never give up part way – I had started, so I would finish. Not completing was never a real option. If I didn't do what I had originally set out to do I would be a failure, and I couldn't live with that. So I pushed myself harder and harder.

Audrey, our social worker, also appreciated the difficulties I was experiencing and offered time and support. Although Ian and I had discontinued mainstream fostering when I went to university, we began to work with the Family Link service, a scheme for families who had a child with disabilities: its foster carers offered respite care to a child who normally lived with his or her own family, giving parents a break from the constant caring role while providing siblings with some valuable time with mum and dad.

Because I had a background in nursing I felt able to offer respite care to a child with complex needs or requiring nursing care. The family with whom we were linked wanted only one Saturday a month. They had experienced difficulties with their child enduring extended periods in hospital many miles away, leaving dad and the other child trying to keep home, school and work on an even keel. When we became involved we were able to provide a valuable space each month for them.

This kind of work still meant that we had regular progress meetings with both the Family Link social worker and the social worker who had originally done our fostering assessments. So Audrey came to our house on many occasions.

Over the years I had talked with Audrey about some of the things that were happening to me, and shared a little more of my history. She knew the bare bones from our assessment visits, but before her very eyes she was seeing the impact on my life of historic abuse. Audrey had some appreciation of the many facets of abuse and its results. She had worked within social services for a long time so she had a lot of experience. She also knew the theory of abuse and how it devastated its victims.

Audrey was concerned about how I was feeling. She was aware of the toll that my journey was taking on me. She was also amazed at how I had looked after the babies we fostered in addition to all the other things I was doing.

Often though when we were together I ended up in tears as she empathised with me. I described to her how I cried so much, and she said, 'What you could do is watch a soppy film. The family will take less notice of you that way and it will give you a legitimate excuse to cry.' This was a useful tip and occasionally I did just that – watched and cried.

But Audrey also advised me of something that changed my perspective and in a small way contributed to the start of my recovery. She gave me a strategy for identifying just how bad things were, or alternatively how well I was doing: 'Get some paper or your diary and write the day down in half-hour slots. During the day, look at the time and check how you have been feeling. Plot every half-hour on your chart, putting either a tick because you have coped OK or a cross because you haven't coped.' She encouraged me to check one day against another and view the pattern of ticks and crosses, and to look for an increase in ticks and fewer crosses. This served me well. I began to see that, although things were tough, not every minute was bad. In fact for half an hour at a time sometimes I would not think about abuse at all. I felt I was making progress.

Generally others had no idea about the state of our marriage. But I began to apply the same reasoning to our marriage that I did to my personal illness and feelings. I noticed that things between Ian and me were not always bad. There were times when we chatted and laughed, even some times when our intimacy was successful. It gave me hope.

The counselling was a great help in supporting me through the court case. After the court case was over I took a break, but I continued with my studies and gained a very respect-able result in my degree and research.

Around the time I graduated, Ian and I were invited by a friend at church to a course called 'Keeping Marriages Healthy'. It seemed quite ironic that we were going to try to keep our marriage healthy when in reality it was ailing desperately. The course was led by a couple we had not met before so we felt less threatened, although two of our church friends were going too.

So each Sunday for eight weeks we went along to try to keep our marriage healthy! At some stage each week we went off as couples into various corners of the rather large room to discuss how the week's topic was relevant to us. We were encouraged to see how we could apply some of the principles we were learning to our own specific situation and plan how to use them in the coming week.

For Ian and me this really was hard work. Sometimes we would get stuck on one thing, and often we would be having a quiet but strong disagreement in our corner. Other couples seemed to be chatting intensely and occasionally laughing while we were at it hammer and tongs. We never made plans for the coming week!

The leaders also encouraged us to have a set time during the week to review things and talk. We never did that either in the whole of the eight weeks! Talking was often so fraught and hurtful that we couldn't bear to bring anything up unless forced to by yet another argument. We learned quite a lot about what the other one liked and needed but it didn't seem to make a significant difference.

In my professional life I began to work my way up, having now gained my degree. I held a responsible post with a large national children's charity and work was going well. At home we continued to rub along and so I thought that was how it would stay. However, after the excitement and challenge of a new job wore off a little, I realised that I needed someone to talk to again. I began to think about how to find another counsellor.

The other fact I considered was that this time I wanted to see someone who was a Christian. I had begun to think about the fact that the person who had abused me was my pastor. I felt that this had a bearing on my feelings about the power he had over me. I didn't know how it all tied in, but I thought it might relate to my feelings about God and also my dad. But I didn't know who I could talk to.

Before I had started the process of prosecution I had, aside from the seminar, called The Churches' Child Protection Advisory Service. I had many questions about how to proceed, and they had given me lots of advice and information which helped me in my decision about whether or not to go to the police. At the end of the conversation they gave me the names and telephone numbers of some counselling centres in my area. One was in the city where I worked. I called them and made a self-referral, giving simple details of name, address and telephone number, and they told me that someone would be in touch.

It wasn't long before I was sitting in a counselling room again. Although there was a lot to tell about where I was up to in my journey, the counsellor and I soon developed a rapport and I was relieved to have a sounding board and an outlet for my feelings. The talking and exploring of ideas were so helpful. I often had the experience of 'a penny dropping' as I described an event or a feeling. It might have been something that troubled me and had put me in turmoil for weeks but, as I began to talk, things would come out of my mouth that I had no idea I was going to say, things that helped me understand what was going on.

Counselling is often described as a 'safe place' and I actually experienced that safety – whatever I said was never condemned and I was never 'told off'. Nothing was off limits. It was a great lesson for me in acceptance. I could talk about feelings that I felt were 'unchristian'. I could let out some of the desires I would never tell another living soul. I was not rejected, told to repent or regarded as a lesser person. It was an amazing feeling.

But after six months of regular meetings with the counsellor I was completely 'talked out'. I knew that I was still not well, but I wanted to take a break. It was very hard actively working on issues and facing feelings and trying to tie it all up with the past. There were often times when I wished I could go back to how things had been. I was exhausted. Battered. My mind would not let it go. Abuse lived with me. It was relentless.

But I knew that, however desperately I wished it, things would never be the same again. Too much had been exposed; too many harsh words had been exchanged within our marriage. My relationship with Ian would never be how it was.

One of the questions that I repeatedly asked of each of the counsellors I saw was, 'How will I know when it's all gone?' There wasn't a clear-cut answer. They couldn't give me a simple formula. I was disappointed.

I gave myself a break but it wasn't long before I was back again. This time I saw a different counsellor, Julie. She and her husband had led the marriage course. I was comfortable with her. The arrangement suited me, but it also led on to a different type of conversation. I spoke about our marriage at considerable length. I talked a lot about Ian, criticising him and saying I was disappointed in him. Actually I was furious with him – it all came out.

At home I never spoke about the counselling. No-one entered into that space. Ian would sometimes ask if the session was OK when I arrived home. My evasive response was, 'Yes, it was fine.'

11 'You need to forgive'

Aileen was a friend and colleague of Dot, the woman in our church with whom I had been praying when I was depression-free. Often the three of us would meet for prayer. We forged a strong bond, and so later when Dot moved to the south of England Aileen and I continued to meet.

On one of those occasions we took ourselves off to a monastery for a couple of days. We wanted to be quiet, pray and have some time to reflect together. One day we were sitting in a small room together. I had been reading from the book of Romans, in which Paul speaks of the fact there is absolutely nothing that can prevent God's love from reaching a person:

> For I am convinced that neither death nor life, neither angels nor demons, neither the present nor the future, nor any powers, neither height nor depth, nor anything else in all creation, will be able to separate us from the love of God that is in Christ Jesus our Lord (Romans 8:38–39).

It was familiar to me, a piece of theology that I believed, though I had never really felt God's love. However that morning I took a step nearer. I lay prostrate on the floor and allowed the words to sink in. Nothing else. No shaft of light. No baptism of peace. Just words resting in my mind.

We also developed a larger group of women who met together quarterly to pray. This was a particularly exciting time of spiritual development and understanding for me. The group grew and we continued to meet for several years.

When I was ill for the second time, initially we still met for prayer and I played an active part in planning and facilitating the women's group. It was during one of my meetings with Aileen that she gave me a book to read. She had found it particularly helpful and we had spoken about it.

The content of the book, though interesting, was not in itself earth-shattering. However what happened as I read was an earth-shattering experience for me. I felt an inner conviction that God was saying to me that I needed to forgive two people. Now I knew a lot about Christian principles and values from the influences and teaching I had imbibed from the Bible over the years, so what I was reading was not new to me. I understood the writer as he explained about forgiveness. I agreed with him on this. But this 'voice' impressed on me the necessity to forgive someone who had hurt Ian and me, and someone whom I absolutely loathed and despised. My knowledge of forgiveness was purely academic faced with the Herculean task ahead. I now had to put it all into practice.

The first person was the senior pastor of the church we had left. Although we were on amicable terms, there were times when I meditated on the hurt and betrayal caused by the decisions that church had taken. I had been so deeply upset at seeing the impact of those decisions on Ian. And in my mind there had been injustice in how the financial implications had been resolved. Other leaders in the church had not taken any of the flak: my perception was that Ian had been singled out.

When I reconsidered all this, I acknowledged that I needed to forgive the man I held responsible. I prayed and I had a feeling of peace. It all felt right.

The other person whom God was saying I needed to forgive was the man who had sexually abused me. This was a shock! 'Hey God, this is not fair. I am ill, I am struggling to care for my family, I have bouts of immense physical and emotional pain and you want me to *forgive* him – just like that?'

This 'injustice' stayed with me for several days. My mind was a whirl. I remembered many individual instances of abuse. I recalled how Ian and I had come up against sexual difficulties in our marriage before any of the depression. I contemplated how things might have been without abuse in my life. I wondered what kind of person I would have turned out to be without the events that had marred my life. It felt like I was a toddler having a tantrum: 'No, I don't want to do this!'

But deep down I knew that for a Christian there were certain basic principles of faith. One of the things I held dear was the knowledge that I could approach God and ask him for forgiveness for anything I had done. But now the shoe was on the other foot. It seemed to me that God was asking me to forgive the impossible. Part of me was still stamping my feet and saying, 'No, this is just not possible.' However, another part of me knew this was right.

I was utterly convinced by the things I knew from the Bible, especially the prayer that Jesus taught in Matthew chapter six that had a proviso attached. For me to be forgiven my wrongs, I needed to forgive others.[1] I thought hard about Jesus' death and the significance of a loving Father sending his sinless Son to die for all sin, which included the crimes against me. I realised that God had made it possible for *any* sin to be forgiven, and that I was being held back from being free of the abuse if I continued to hold on to unforgiveness.

Although it was quite clear in the light of this that forgiving seemed the 'sensible' approach, I considered that there were possibly some exceptions. Surely this was one of them? In my mind the damage inflicted on me justified my reluctance even to entertain forgiving. I battled it out with God.

Finally I realised that this was a choice, one of the most difficult of my life. God wasn't going to bang me over the head with a big stick if I felt this was a bridge too far, but if I was in fact convinced that it was what I needed to do, then it had to be wholehearted. I made the choice, but having reached a decision I wondered how to carry it out. Did this mean meeting Roy? Did I have to tell him I'd forgiven him? Did it involve him at all? Could I pray and it would all be OK?

I hatched a plan. I felt that if I prayed alone it would not be real. It seemed to me that I needed a witness. If someone else was with me and knew that I had said the words 'I forgive Roy', that would give me reassurance that it was real. It would be over and done with and I would be able to leave it at that. But the problem was, who could witness my prayer? Who could I talk to about this? I had not spoken to people outside the family (apart from professionals) about any of my experiences. I was aware that there could be some embarrassment for both myself and the person I talked to. I was in a newish church and was unsure as to whether I could offload to people there. But then it became obvious. Aileen had provided the book: Aileen was the one I could trust.

I arranged to see Aileen at her house. She was some years older than me and did things in a formal way. When I arrived there was a tray set with a small plate and two coffee mugs. We talked while the kettle was on; she placed some biscuits on the plate and put ground coffee into a small cafetière. She took it through to a sitting area between the kitchen and the dining room. There were two low, old-fashioned chairs and we sat down, Aileen drawing up a small table with the tray as we did so.

I watched as Aileen pressed the plunger that pushed all the coffee granules to the bottom of the pot. I was glad of the formalities. I didn't really want coffee at that point but it meant that while she was busy with that she wasn't concentrating on me. It delayed the inevitable. But after we were settled Aileen turned, looked straight at me and asked, 'What was it you wanted to see me about?'

It wasn't too much of a problem to talk about the abuse but I didn't want to overload Aileen with information she didn't need to know. On the other hand I wanted her to know that this was a major step for me. I also wanted her to appreciate that, although I had made this decision with no coercion and in fact with no-one else's knowledge, nevertheless it was far from easy for me.

In a few short sentences I talked about having been abused, who the person was and his relationship to our family, and my recognition that the depression and my current difficulties were directly related to my history. I referred to the book she had lent me and how through it God had impressed on me the need to forgive. I also explained that I had the feeling that someone witnessing my prayer would somehow enhance my actions and decision.

She listened attentively. She showed no shock or surprise but nodded and looked at me intently. I felt accepted and believed. She didn't ask me any questions until I had finished, and then she simply said, 'Would you like to pray now?' Oh dear, the time had come. Yes I wanted to and no I didn't want to. I had no idea what I was going to say. I think deep down I wanted her to take the lead; I wanted her to do it. But this was my call, my decision, my prayer to pray.

I sat holding the wooden chair arm with my left hand, and then used my forefinger to stroke the wood. I was looking hard at it. There were beautiful grains in the wood which was probably oak. It was smooth and shiny from many other hands holding it. Aileen was in the chair a little to my right but at an angle. She was poised for prayer: her hands lay in her lap and she sat fairly upright. She was quiet and so was I. I really wanted to do this. If I did it would be another box I could tick. It would be another issue faced, and then surely God would soon take all the pain away and I would be well again.

My heart was pounding and my mouth was dry. I remembered having a dry mouth before but on a much happier occasion: on the day I got married. As my dad and I had sat in the bridal car outside our family home I had said, 'Dad, my mouth is so dry I'll have to have a drink.' The memory flashed through my mind, but then I realised I needed to think about the present and how to pray the most difficult prayer I had ever uttered. The longer the silence, the more difficult it became. I just couldn't get any words to come out of my mouth.

Aileen sat and waited. This was something no-one else could do for me. I really had to do it myself. I began to pray, 'Dear Lord, help me to forgive Roy for all the things he did to me, in Jesus' name. Amen.' Just a few simple words, but I had done it and the amazing thing was that I really meant it. No comets flew across the sky; no cosmic affirmation resulted. There was just a huge sense of relief that I had actually done it! Aileen and I looked at each other and enjoyed the moment.

As a young adult I had been a fairly consistent person. My life did not have highs and lows until I became depressed. I didn't dwell on things, and forged through life rather like a train at full speed. Occasionally, as I said earlier, there would be something that made me really angry and I would fly into a rage. It was always something insignificant and my anger was completely out of proportion to the cause. I didn't give it much thought because immediately after the outburst I would want to forget it, without acknowledging any hurt I might have inflicted, expecting everything to revert to normal. These rages had usually been directed at Ian. I could contain myself admirably with others but I would flare up at home. There seemed to be neither rhyme nor reason for this.

This anger troubled me. I felt guilty about it for it was not how a Christian should behave. When I was a child and a young person one of the teachings I had imbibed was that anger was a sin. There was nothing in my upbringing that had helped me develop ways of showing anger appropriately or even acknowledging that it was OK to be angry and feel such emotions. So I grew up thinking that anger wasn't OK and if you have it you can't express it at all, and also that you can't talk about it because actually you shouldn't have any in the first place! As an adult I was ill prepared to deal with rage and so I gave it little thought until about 1990. I justified it because, after all, it didn't happen very often.

I had recovered from depression first time round but the feelings of anger only seemed to be increasing. I realised that I was actually a very angry person indeed and I wanted help. I thought back over my life and realised that I had been angry for as long as I could remember. I had on one occasion made arrangements to see a mature person in a senior position in the church where Ian was still in leadership. I explained about the anger and that I was troubled and needed some advice. But I was shocked at his response. He laughed and said, 'You, angry? I can't imagine that!' End of conversation. There was no further comment, no offer to pray with me. I was confused. 'Perhaps I'm OK; maybe it's not as bad as I thought,' I reasoned, but deep down I knew it was.

Nothing changed except that anxiety about anger was added to the equation. Occasionally I had prayed about the anger over the years but it had made no difference. I was even angry with God. One day I was walking by the canal with the dog and I was in a rage with God about it all:

'You know about this anger and you could take it away. I have *asked* you to, so why don't you?' I heard no answer.

During a conversation with one of the women at church the topic turned towards depression. She said that it could be caused by unresolved anger. I felt angry! It was OK for me to identify that I was angry but I didn't want to hear it from someone else.

But I knew the problem well. I was angry that I had been abused. I was angry at the injustices in my life. I was angry that I had been neglected. I was angry that I had been so restricted as a child and teenager. I was angry that no-one had asked me the right questions so that I could have told them. I was angry that no-one seemed to care. I was angry that adults had such power. And every time I felt justifiably angry about other things in life, this was added to the store because I had been so conditioned to ignore it. But occasionally it burst the dam and released the pressure for a while – until the next time. Like a volcano I would erupt, leaving debris around, and then almost immediately be right back behaving rationally again.

The anger that had been suppressed over many years had built up. Many of my tears were angry. Inner seething came out in hurtful retorts, rebuffing Ian, shouting. I was one extremely angry person. Until I forgave.

Within a couple of weeks of forgiving Roy I knew that something very powerful had happened. My levels of anger had reduced dramatically. The reservoirs of pent-up anger that had never been allowed to be expressed were drained almost dry.

There were some occasions when I realised that I felt a deep anger, but knowing and recognising it was a huge step forward.

Over the years we had acquired a number of pots, dishes and other bits of crockery that were cracked, old and ready for the bin. They sat in a large plastic box outside. The next time I was angry I held it in and waited until it was safe, with the boys at school and no neighbours in their gardens. I took some crockery to the bottom of our garden and threw it up against the wall. Cup after cup shattered and fell onto the path below. It was a great release. I swept up the debris and put it all in the bin. This was the first of several occasions of smashing therapy!

After a few sessions of ridding myself of the residual anger of the past, I knew that the angry demonstrations were over. I had a new perspective. I understood that anger is OK and that showing anger in the right way is healthy. The steps in my progress were slow but I was gaining some ground.

Forgiveness stood me in good stead to withstand another difficulty. Three months after the court case I received a telephone call. The boys had not arrived home from school, and I was alone. It was Margaret.

'Hi, are you OK?' she asked.

'Yes, fine,' I replied, although that was far from the truth.

'Is anyone with you?' she asked.

'No, but everyone will be home soon, I expect,' I replied.

'Then I've got some news for you,' she said. 'Sheila's friend has phoned her because there is something in the evening papers that she thought we should know about.'

'Oh?' I said weakly.

'Roy has died in prison,' she said. We were both quiet but then she asked, 'Are you OK?' In the short quiet space I was thinking about how he had come to be in prison. Immediately I took the blame, thinking, 'It was you who put him there, Greta.' I replied to Margaret, 'Yes I'm OK', and we each put down the phone.

Initially I was emotional. The guilt I felt was immense. My tears were inexplicable, given the circumstances. But then I began to rationalise what I had heard and realised just why he had been in prison. 'It's not because of you; it's because of his own actions. And you have forgiven him.'

12 'I think we need to talk to somebody'

My new job involved recruiting and training volunteers who would be suitable to visit and befriend children in the care system. When I arrived for the first day there were no desks, the telephone engineer was still installing lines, and the office boasted a lone photocopier and little more. But I loved challenge and new things, so I got stuck in.

Coping with depression, work and home was challenging but I treated them like I did everything else: I just got on with it, pushing myself all the time. I didn't tell anyone at work about how I was feeling or anything about my past. Work was a cover-up, hiding the real me. Development, challenge and innovation began to mask despair and depression.

But the clandestine inner journey often tripped me up because a migraine would attack and lay me low. And the irritable bowel symptoms would make their presence felt. It seemed that a physical display of illness was shouting out the psychological damage.

Managing it all was a little tricky at times, but after many months of intensive work I crashed more spectacularly. And this time I was the victim of my own success. The project I managed had grown and grown until a number of volunteers were helping out. At this point the regional director wanted me to take on another member of staff so that I could manage even more people. It sounded exciting, but the remit now also involved me working five days a week instead of four.

I hadn't worked full-time since our children had been born. But as they grew I took on more and more hours. University was usually only three days a week, and then I could work at home while the boys were occupied or asleep. Full-time was a step I needed to consider carefully, and so over the Christmas period I thought about what I could manage.

The regional director was pressing for an answer after the Christmas break so I said I would work the five days. I soon missed being at home each Friday, and the weekends weren't long enough to fit in all I needed to do. Weeknights were taken up with helping the boys, Sunday with church. I was on a merry-go-round except it wasn't very merry. I would often say, 'Stop the world, I want to get off.'

As the weeks went by the extra work and responsibilities, added to my home life and illness, started to drain me. I dipped lower and lower. Up to this point I had had only fleeting conversations with doctors about what was going on, usually added on to conversations about 'real' conditions. Now I didn't mind telling the doctor that I had a pain in my abdomen. And he rightly identified irritable bowel syndrome as a telltale sign of unhealthy emotions. I asked another doctor about migraine and she agreed that it too could have emotional triggers. But I never had a serious conversation about being depressed and any possible treatment.

By now I was demotivated, lethargic and completely flat emotionally, and knew I couldn't continue. I planned some time off work. There had been reorganisation and the new manager was easy to talk to and very understanding. I spoke with him about how I was feeling, explaining some of what I had been through. I told him that I needed to take some time off work. I planned things in a very orderly way so that my small staff group would be able to carry on, left my desk and went to the doctor.

As I've already said, my particular brand of Christian upbringing did not allow for depression; my vocabulary didn't include it, but the stark reality was that I had it.

My attitude towards depression was cynical. How could I possibly be treated if part of me was intolerant of people who were depressed? What could tablets do in addition to all the effort I was putting in to free myself from the trauma? If I decided to go for treatment how could I explain antidepressants to Ian? What was the prevailing attitude of the church? Were antidepressants addictive? How long would I need to take them? How did they work?

My mind tossed between 'do I?' and 'don't I?'. This was a major decision, totally new territory. I had known others who had taken antidepressants, but I felt that I should be strong enough to pull through on my own. But the most persistent thought was that a Christian on antidepressants spelt 'failure'.

After a few weeks of turning all these things over in my mind I went to the doctor. I talked to him of the years I had been living with depression. I told him just a little of what I felt had generated my prolonged illness.

Since we had changed doctors after Yorkshire I had always seemed to be 'in the way' when I had an appointment. It felt as if the doctor couldn't wait to get me out through the door, and that he was unconcerned and uninterested. Following my explanation my feelings were confirmed. After I had bared my soul to him he turned to me and said, 'I suppose you want some pills?' I was shattered but I also felt indignant. He had no idea what it had taken for me to reach this decision or how his insensitive remark had completely destroyed any confidence I had in him.

So I was prescribed antidepressants for the first time ever and the doctor gave me a sick note. But I still wanted to do it my way. I was off work and, although I had been to the gym a couple of times a week for the previous few months, I now went every morning. I had read that endorphins would lift my mood. I reasoned that exercise combined with the medication would see me well in no time.

The doctor told me it could take up to three or four weeks before I felt any benefit from the medication. So at the end of three weeks I was not surprised when I felt no different, although I did think the gym would have helped. After weeks four and five I thought there was no hope. My manager and I would chat occasionally on the phone. He was genuinely interested in me, didn't mention work, and put no pressure on me at all. He just wanted me to be well. We spoke about whether or not I should ask the doctor for another type of medication. But I decided against this because I would need to start all over again and the last five weeks would all have been for nothing.

But just a few days later I noticed that I felt slightly better. It seemed that the pit I was in had a ladder attached to the side and I was able to step up onto the bottom rung. My situation remained the same but something within me had changed slightly. It was not the 'happy-pill' feeling that some people speak of; it was the ability to cope better, not to be so irritable, not to be quite so low in mood. It was the difference between needing to be off work and being fit to return. So, following a total of about nine weeks, I returned to work and got things up and running at full speed again. But there was a change. I negotiated to work four days a week and let the other staff pick up the extra hours.

Although we hid many things from our family and friends, Ian and I had reached stalemate. We had changed and were now managing to be civil and friendly with each other. The hurt and anger in our conversations had been reduced. It appeared that we had both resigned ourselves to the fact that was how our future life together would be. I had determined I would stay for the boys so that they would not have to split their time or loyalties between two separated parents. But I was no longer making any effort to improve things between us. I had tried. The marriage input we had received had produced only a temporary effect. Such was the deep hurt and damage that it would take much more time to get to the bottom of it all than the marriage course could offer. I decided that, rather than have more arguments, I would focus on myself. I so wanted to be well.

Because we communicated only on the surface I had no idea what Ian was thinking. Although I had benefited enormously from counselling I had never really considered the possibility of us going together. I didn't ask Ian if he would. I actually wanted the suggestion to come from him, if at all. I didn't want to be the instigator because often it's not easy facing up to issues, and if we were to go together and things became a little tricky I realised it would give Ian the opportunity to say to me, 'This was all your idea. I didn't want it.' However Ian had also taken a decision: he didn't want to live like this any longer. He remembered how our marriage had been, how we used to communicate so well. He was saddened by how we were living now and all his thinking finally kicked him into action.

We were tidying up in the kitchen one evening after our meal. Ian was sorting the pots and loading the dishwasher and I was wiping the work surfaces and putting things into cupboards. We were silent but it wasn't a hostile silence. As we finished Ian turned to me and said, 'I think we need to talk to somebody.'

Subconsciously I was ready to hear this. But I was unaware that I was ready until I had actually heard it. On one level my mind saw the relationship as dead and almost buried, but on another I recognised that this was just what I had been waiting for. I had never spoken about my counselling sessions to Ian. He never understood the issues I was beginning to understand, and how childhood tied into adult life. But what he could now see was that some things were different and working better for me. He himself was desperately unhappy; he wanted to salvage our marriage and show his commitment.

I responded immediately. From somewhere deep within, although not consciously, I had made a plan. I too wanted to get our marriage back on track. I wanted our sons to have parents who were a partnership and not just two separate individuals.

'I'll phone the Light House,' I said.[1] That was the start of us building together again.

We told the boys that we were going for counselling, explaining briefly that we needed to talk to someone who could help us put right some things that had gone wrong in our marriage. The boys said little, just accepted the situation. We then began a journey of eleven months in which we explored all our pent-up feelings from both perspectives.

Our first appointment happened quite quickly. We saw Julie again, but together this time. All through the years of struggling I had felt that Ian was on one side of a fence and I was on the other, but I was also in the middle, trying to explain to him what it was like to be me! But from the first counselling session the feeling of support was incredible. The counsellor was able to help Ian understand. She took the responsibility from me of explaining the damage of abuse. She talked about the validity of some of my responses. She helped us say things to each other that had escalated into arguments when we had tried to say them on our own. It was safe for me to say things to Ian that needed to be said but which I had been fearful of saying when there were just the two of us trying to get out of our mess. The counsellor's presence gave me courage. In an amazing way she gave Ian the ability to listen and to begin to understand the effect of childhood sexual abuse. I felt that here was someone who was on my side. Although the previous counselling had helped greatly, I had always struggled with a feeling of being alone. Now someone was on my side and able to explain to Ian how he had missed the point and needed to grasp some basic principles. We had been broken by it all but were now beginning to mend.

The three of us met together for many months and talked. We brought up things that had previously been unsafe to mention, and laughed at other things, and sometimes the three of us cried. We were digging out old hurts, pulling up roots of feelings that had buried themselves deep down below the surface. Wounds were opened so that they could be cleaned and treated. And Ian and I were getting closer.

My job at the time involved working with young people on the autistic spectrum. I was staggered as I read about Asperger's syndrome to 'see' Ian in the pages. Although undiagnosed and unrecognised, here were many symptoms that I could identify: the social aspects, the adherence to routines, the sensitivity to noise: all were features evident within our marriage. But more importantly I realised why we were experiencing difficulties and why Ian had been unable to speak up for me when I had wanted anyone but Roy to marry us. The lack of empathy was a grave problem but no fault of Ian's. He was simply not able to put himself in my shoes or appreciate how I was feeling. It was a complete revelation. Ian and I read together so that we could under-stand it all and make improvements. It was an important part of moving forward in step together.

We made rapid progress. Ian was a willing learner and developed a huge amount of knowledge, using it to change his perspective. He deeply regretted not being able to support me in the way I had expected and needed. In turn I deeply regretted the wall of resentment that I had built when feeling unsupported. Many times we apologised to each other for different things that had been said or done.

We were growing up. At the end of each session we left with more positive things to think about.

The counselling centre ran on client donations. We had discussed the amount we felt we should contribute for each session. Ian took out his chequebook and at the end of every couple of sessions he would write a cheque for the amount we had allocated. Occasionally he would show some hesitation, mulling over the cost in his mind. I could tell what he was thinking.

We had never discussed divorce, not even in our worst moments. It was another of those words that were not in our vocabulary. It was never an option. We never even joked about divorce. But I was feeling much more confident about everything now, even about addressing sensitive things. Once as he hesitated when writing the cheque, I knew he was probably wondering how many more sessions he would need to budget for, mentally adding up the sums. So I said, 'Well, Ian, it's cheaper than a divorce!' Ian was a little taken aback, but he glanced across, looked me in the eye and, realising that it was a joke, just smiled. I knew then that we would make it.

13 'I just feel like I want to scream'

In the summer of 2001 I wrote a special list in my journal. There were days when I felt really well, days when I was mostly well, and some days when I was far from well, but I was recovering. I was noticing the differences. I put two columns: 'before' and 'now'. I could identify how things had changed. From being uninterested in work and leisure I was now beginning to feel much more motivated. From being exhausted my body now felt more rested. The irritation had given way to a more laid-back approach. The hopeless moments were fewer. And wanting to die was certainly not as prominent as it had been. From constantly wanting space from everyone, I was happy within the family mêlée. I didn't consider everything to be drudgery, for I was much more content.

Around that time Ian and I took our youngest son, Nathan, to visit Adam who was living in the south of England. It was a bank holiday weekend and we stayed in a hotel near Adam's flat. On the Saturday we went to a nearby town to have a look round the shops. Ian and I saw a picture by Rolf Harris which we considered buying. There was a little rain but nothing that stopped us enjoying ourselves. Claire, Adam's girlfriend, Nathan and I went to see an ice show on the Saturday evening while Ian and Adam ate and chatted together at the hotel. We found a lively church on the Sunday. All in all it was a great weekend.

Following breakfast on the Monday, Ian and I left the hotel to pick up Adam and Claire to go to Brighton. It was a lovely journey through several very beautiful villages and along scenic country roads. Once we got to Brighton we queued to get into the town and drove along the sea-front and then circled around trying to find somewhere to park.

After eventually finding a remote car park we caught a bus into the centre of town, walked along the beach and bought ice creams. We sat in the sun and chatted together. And then we went onto the pier.

At the end of Brighton Pier there are several fairground rides. Some are quite tame but others too scary to contemplate. However there was no contemplating necessary for the younger ones. They wanted to have a go on a particular ride with two huge metal arms that swung in opposite directions, taking them higher and higher until they were upside down. The passengers were suspended for a few seconds, and then down came the arms having crossed over precariously at the top. There was no way I was going on that ride; dodgems, yes, but crossing metal arms was a complete 'no-no' for me. Yet the fairground turned out to be the highlight of my day.

I had sometimes said to Ian, 'I just feel like I want to scream.' Or another way I sometimes described it was, 'I feel there is a scream inside me.' Early in my journey of discovering the impact of abuse I had come across a book called *Releasing the Scream*.[1] I had no doubt but that this was one for my reading list – a writer who could identify with some of the things I was experiencing. It was another confirmation for me that I was not going mad but that other people too had felt this urge within them.

And now Ian and I could talk more freely about feelings and things that were going on internally and individually. He now knew about the significance of the scream, for we had both realised how the scream was probably yet another area of pent-up anger against the abuser, a deep frustration because no-one had detected and stopped what had gone on when I was a child. It was my child voice that wanted to shout 'STOP'. We appreciated that getting rid of The Scream was a genuine problem.

I had often wondered how I could get to scream somewhere. Was there a field far enough away from anyone where I could go and scream without attracting police-car sirens from all corners? And if I found somewhere, could I get a scream out? How loud would I be able to scream? And would it help? I concluded that it really wasn't safe to try it. There was nowhere I would feel comfortable that was out of earshot. So reluctantly I shelved the idea.

But now on Brighton Pier I had the perfect opportunity. The family wanted to go on the scary ride. And I wanted them to go! They had emptied wallets, handbag and various contents of their pockets into my willing hands. As they went towards the ride I stood by the barrier fence and said, 'You ride and I'll scream for you.' It was ideal. They didn't have a clue what was going on but Ian and I looked at each other and waited for them to be flung into space. I screamed. I screamed again. I screamed at full volume. I stood within earshot of dozens of people but no-one took the least bit of notice. It was such a relief and a release.

Shortly after this, with new management arrangements at work, there were two separate teams being supervised by the same manager. We had a good working relationship: team meetings together and we sometimes socialised as well. The manager decided to do a team day and someone suggested visiting a theme park. It seemed a silly idea as we were all much older than the usual clientele. But I saw it as another opportunity to do some more screaming therapy.

On the day it turned out that we were a group of just four women. We had taken a picnic so we joked about how many more samosas we each could scoff in the absence of the male members of our team. But before the picnic we needed to get on with the business of riding the pirate ship, the roller coaster Oblivion, the log flume and all the other rides.

I went on all of them except one. But on each one I was able to release some more of my inner scream. The park was made for screams: it was legitimate to scream, it was *expected* that there would be screams. I screamed as I was turned upside down, screamed as I got soaked, screamed in the dark, screamed as I was flung into the air. I screamed and screamed and screamed.

14 'A year of Jubilee'

My down days were getting much less frequent and I was managing my emotions much better.

I went to Ellel Ministries for a healing retreat and spent three days in the company of people who were feeling hurt and pain similar to mine.[1] We were each allocated two individuals who would talk and pray with us between the group sessions of Bible teaching. For those few days I was cocooned, surrounded by TLC and people who could empathise. And it helped me to focus on God and his healing presence.

It was all coming together. Each type of help and support was playing a part in helping me to understand and overcome the deep impact of abuse. I was gaining ground and becoming very much more optimistic.

Another birthday was approaching: I would soon be fifty. It felt significant for more than one reason. Ian said to me, 'This is going to be a year of Jubilee.' Now I knew that in the Bible the year of Jubilee was a time of celebration when slaves were set free.[2] I thought about what that could mean for me: freedom! I wondered how it would happen.

Ian and I talked about how to celebrate. I had decided that, in view of all the problems we had overcome, and also recognising that birthdays had been significantly lacking in my childhood, I was going to have the mother of all parties. And I did. I wanted a barn dance with a live band, balloons and a cake. I invited church, family and friends. We danced and laughed. I blew out the candles. Everyone sang 'Happy Birthday' to me. And I glowed from inside!

I came home floating on a cloud. I was fifty with three handsome sons and about to become a grandparent for the first time. I had a supportive and loving husband. Things were on the up.

Over the months of counselling and talking together my respect for Ian had grown. I could see he was desperately wanting to get things right. He valued our marriage and wanted it back on track. However as our relationship improved it wasn't just as before; in fact, we were in a much better place. And I realised that something had happened in me: I was beginning to love again.

Several months later I came home from work to find Ian very excited. He showed me something that had come in the post: 'We've been invited to Lucy's fiftieth birthday party and we're going.'

Mervyn and Lucy were involved in evangelism and we had known them since Adam was just a few months old. We came to know them because they had visited the small Yorkshire town where we had lived. We had become firm friends and had enjoyed many good times together. However, over the years when we had been having difficulties there had been many times when we had chosen to isolate ourselves, turning down offers of evenings out and not inviting people to our home as we had neither the energy nor the inclination to socialise. We kept in touch with cards and news at Christmas but we hadn't seen Mervyn or been to the church where he was a minister for a number of years.

But now we were planning to see them. Mervyn had arranged a surprise party for Lucy, hiring a large venue in their nearest city. They were from farming stock and had many friends in the Yorkshire and Lancashire farming community, a number of whom would be present.

Ian and I booked a two-night break in a hotel not far from the party venue. We had been asked to arrive at a specific time and gathered along with many others in a side room. We could hear a hum of voices in the next room but were unaware of what was going on. We chatted to some people we knew while we waited.

Then the man at the door began to call people forward and usher them into the next room. The majority of the guests had been seated ready for Lucy's arrival, but others of us were secreted away to give her even more of a surprise. Couple after couple were called through and then our turn came. We were taken into a very large room full of tables with guests seated round them. Our names were announced and we went forward to where Lucy was standing, greeting all her surprise guests. People began to clap, there was a lot of noise, and we chatted briefly before taking our places.

During the evening we were able to catch up with lots of friends. It was a party, the like of which I had never been to before. We did a lot of singing, and people took the mike and spoke about their friendship over the years with both Lucy and Mervyn. At the end of the evening we were standing singing together in worship. Inside I felt something stirring.

During the years of desolation Ian would sometimes say to me, 'I wonder when we will go into ministry again.' This was something in which I had no interest. If we never did any ministry again, as far as I was concerned, it would be too soon! Church work at that level was totally off my agenda. 'I don't want to talk about it,' I would respond.

But by the end of the party I was feeling a stirring of interest. I did want to be involved; I did want to do whatever God had planned for me. I was experiencing the beginning of a turnaround.

The next morning we went to Mervyn and Lucy's church. Their meeting place was part of a converted barn on a farm. It wasn't very big and, as many people had stayed over following the party, we were all packed in like sardines. Mervyn and Lucy were among the last to arrive and they greeted us all individually as they made their way to the front. Again it was a joyous occasion right from the start. Mervyn greeted and hugged us. We were in tears as he asked, 'What will heaven be like?' What a reunion of friends!

It was an amazing morning. Ian and I had come to a good place of understanding each other over the previous two years and we were again enjoying being together. We had apologised for so many things, forgiven so many hurts. We had started another part of our life together. But this was the icing on the cake. God had a divine way of bringing further healing to us.

We didn't know the preacher; we hadn't met him or heard him speak before, but he stood and pointed at us. He began to describe the dark experience we had been through. He knew because God had revealed it to him that we had struggled. He said things that pinpointed our difficulties and then he gave us something to look forward to. He said, 'The best is yet to come.'

It was two weeks away from my fifty-first birthday. This was indeed a special year – a year of Jubilee!

15 'This is our calling'

We had been in Tenerife for about eight days and had two or three days left before flying home. It was the end of March and we were approaching our thirty-fifth wedding anniversary. We decided to splash out and celebrate early by going to a special restaurant as our anniversary treat.

The menu was astounding. There was camembert in brioche, a fish or meat selection, some delicacies whose identities we had to guess and desserts to die for. We asked for descriptions of what we didn't understand and placed our order.

It was so different from our silver wedding. We were ten years on and had made enormous progress. We chatted over our drinks and commented on the décor. We were relaxed and enjoying beautiful cuisine – we decided we would go the whole hog and have desserts too.

As we waited we started talking about the years we had spent together. I asked Ian, 'What have been the highlights of the last thirty-five years?' He talked about our sons, his love for them and how he had enjoyed their early years, the things we had done as a family and the joy the boys had brought into his life. He described how he loved me, and was so glad that we had come through so much into a different relationship. And then I asked, 'Do you have any regrets?' He didn't have to give it much thought. It was obviously something that was near to the surface and he needed to express it: 'I regret that I didn't support you more when you needed it.' I was deeply touched. My love for Ian was indeed growing.

Since Lucy's birthday we had kept in touch with her and Mervyn and had visited their church again. Lucy and Mervyn had travelled extensively over the years, having initially visited India almost twenty-five years before, soon after we first met them. After visits and discussions they had established a children's home in the south east, in the state of Andhra Pradesh. Over the years they also developed childcare facilities in Nepal, followed by Myanmar and Thailand. When they were not abroad they were travelling locally to raise support and funds for the children's education and clothes and the premises in which the children lived.

Once when we were together Mervyn had made a suggestion to Ian: 'Why don't you come with me to India?' Ian was delighted and they immediately began to plan what they would do and decide when would be the best time of year to visit.

Over the next four years Ian went off to India three times. He formed relationships with people, travelled to different places and was greatly fulfilled in doing Bible teaching and preaching. He absolutely loved being in India.

I had no interest in this apart from supporting Ian in doing what he felt was right for him. He showed me the photos but they meant little to me as I had never met the people or seen the places. I read the e-mails but couldn't relate to them. Still I was happy for him to go whenever he wanted. I would pack his suitcase, drive him to the airport and keep everything at home ticking over while he was away.

In March 2008 I was waiting in the airport car park for a telephone call to say Ian had landed. I was looking forward to seeing him. He had been away for almost three weeks and I had missed him. As we drove home Ian was experiencing a number of conflicting feelings. He was tired from the journey, pleased to see me but also sad at having left friends again. Coming home always entailed a mixture of emotions for him.

Once in the house he immediately opened his suitcase because he wanted to give me some gifts. Opening these gifts from his Indian friends and clothes from the tailor, and talking together, I suddenly felt I had been a part of the trip. I didn't know these people, I couldn't visualise the places, but it all felt familiar to me. So I simply said to Ian, 'Next time you go I will go with you.'

My life was now on an even keel. There were so many areas I could identify that were now sorted out. We had made great progress in our marriage. Each of our sons was now married. So we booked our flights for India. I had suggested that perhaps I could go for a week to try it out and Ian could stay longer. I knew that a week would be long enough for me. But in the end we were in India for nineteen nights and it wasn't a moment too long!

Ian's friends greeted us at the airport with their family members, garlands of flowers in their hands, and a camera to capture our every move. We had arranged a few days' holiday before going to their village, so they took us to our hotel where we could all spend a couple of hours talking. Straight away, Ian's friends became mine. I felt so excited that I had made the trip with him. They loved me and I loved them. I was overwhelmed by it all.

They left us there to rest and take a short holiday, but I couldn't wait to see them again. I had fallen in love with them. But we enjoyed a rest. Each day we were less tired and gaining strength.

One day as we walked along the beach we saw hundreds of tiny crabs, some red and others camouflaged against the sand. I was so excited to see them scuttle down into the sand when we approached. It was such fun. 'Look, over there! Look, there are some more,' I was squealing with delight. I felt really carefree and I knew exactly what was happening. As we were walking on the sand I said to Ian, 'I feel just like a big kid!' God was bringing deep-down healing and giving me a taste of some of the things I had missed as a child. I had been far from carefree then, weighed down with adult responsibility, but now at last the little girl had a chance to squeal and laugh with delight.

Three days later our hosts Suvarna and Prema were back, this time with two of their children, and again they brought garlands to honour us.

We spent the last day of our holiday with their family and they took us to a large park high on a hill overlooking the Bay of Bengal. It was a day of getting to know one another and we shared deeply about our lives. Prema and I cried together and all of us laughed together. Their children were delightful.

After a final night at the hotel we set off to drive south for about four hours to their village. We stopped on the outskirts of Visakhapatnam near the hotel to pick up another two members of their extended family to take with us.

It was a wonderful time, seeing so much of the country and experiencing the Indian customs. Fish were laid out on one side of the dual carriageway to dry; chairs lined the central reservation; washing adorned the trees and fences. Women in colourful saris were bent over in the rice fields while others were crouched, hammering large blocks of stone. Trucks and tractors were full to overflowing with men going to work. Men and boys herded goats and bullocks to better grazing. The towns were crowded with people every-where. Vehicles came at us from every direction, some approaching us head on, using the wrong side of the road. It was mayhem. But I loved it.

We stopped for a snack of bananas, and the children ate rice and curry.

We arrived in Ponguturu to a huge reception of men and women, children, more garlands, more smiles and many, many hugs. The people all knew Ian and, although they didn't speak English, they showed such joy at having us both in their village.

From there we hit the ground running. We dedicated a church, someone's home and a project for widows. We preached in villages and at a large convention and at a pastors' conference. We visited other family members and the home of a Hindu lady who had asked us to pray with her. We travelled by train to another area, and spent time with the orphaned children who lived in Suvarna's home. We shook hundreds of hands.

But none of it seemed remotely onerous. We had the energy to do everything. Most amazingly I didn't have a migraine. It was an incredible experience and I was hooked.

We had been attending a pastors' conference during the day and were preparing for the evening convention meeting. Ian and I had showered and were talking as we changed for our evening meal. As Ian buttoned his shirt I looked across at him from the bed where I was sitting and said, 'This is our calling.' Ian had known for some years that his interest in India was not just a 'nice' thing to do; he knew that God had led him there, but to have me in the frame too was all he could ever have wanted. India had won me over. God was tying up the loose ends of my healing.

Yorkshire had always been the pinnacle of my life, with its awesome scenery and warm, hospitable people. Our children were born there and the lifestyle had suited us well. Yorkshire was a reference point, the place I always looked back on. It had a special place in my heart, and it had been traumatic when we left.

In the quiet of Suvarna and Prema's home as the day was just starting, I said to Ian, 'I never thought I would say this, but this is better than Yorkshire.' Another wound was healing over.

The day came when we had to leave. We were all quietly getting on with things. The men took suitcases to the car and tied them to the roof rack. Prema was preparing food for our journey and the children were pottering about, but no-one was looking forward to the goodbyes. Many people had gathered on the veranda to see us off and the family were going to accompany us to the railway station. We had already made plans for another visit and had spoken to Suvarna about the timing, the heat, the rains and other factors we needed to take into consideration.

We felt that our return visits would happen as often as possible. A deep wish had been born within us to support the developing widows' project. We knew we would be able to teach the group of pastors who were young in the faith. The orphaned children needed funds and we wanted to be part of that too. There was so much happening that resonated with our heartfelt desires.

As we left, both men and women cried, the children wanted to hold on to us, and extended family members too were reluctant to see us go. The team of pastors stood there, all desperately wanting to say something. Amid the sadness I was aware of all the good things that had happened in such a short time. God had been doing so much outwardly that contributed to a bigger picture of healing on the inside.

The scene at the railway station was just as emotional. Suvarna and Prema's children were there, and Ian and I took them to one side to say a special goodbye to them. They had loved and served us in such a wonderful way, respecting and honouring us. They had truly taken us to their hearts. We felt that we had been given three more children to love.

As we stepped onto the train we called out, 'We're coming back; we'll come back. God will bring us back.'

Epilogue

Life is a journey and it brings constant changes. Our perceptions, attitudes and behaviour are not static. Since 1994 I have been on a progressive journey and actively working towards resolving the impact of childhood sexual abuse. I am now in a position to be able to bring positive hope to those who are still in the thick of it, and to those who may be supporting others through their journey. It *is* possible to lay it to one side and get on with life. Even more, it is possible to become whole.

The impact of abuse on every area of my life has been enormous. Spiritually I have been distant and cold. I have felt at times that God has abandoned me. The person who should have been a spiritual mentor to me as a child and teenager was the very one who abused me, so that much of my thinking became completely distorted. Emotionally I fell apart. There were times when running away or, worse still, dying seemed a far better option than trying to keep going. I felt I had no value, that I was unloved and unlovable. I pushed myself to achieve, to find acceptance through 'doing', and had no strategies to deal with any kind of conflict, voice my opinion or stand up for myself. Physically I have endured much pain and have constantly struggled with weight problems.

My mask for many years was a smile. Behind the smile though lay a mass of tangled thoughts and a mixture of emotions. But my journey has untangled them. Through reading, counselling, prayer and writing, I have been helped to take a thread and trace it back to its source, and then do that repeatedly until one by one the threads have been singled out. The smile is now valid, the anger is appropriate, and the feelings are more easily identified. I now know that I am loved. I am developing a true confidence and not just a blustering veneer. I realise that achievements do not make me who I am. I understand that esteem comes from within and not from trying to please everyone around me. I recognise – most of the time – that it's OK not to be perfect! But I still struggle with all these things on various occasions. I am a work in progress, but one day I will be made whole.

The part that forgiveness has played in my overall story has been of immense importance. The power of forgiveness never ceases to amaze me. The impact of forgiveness on resolving my anger was completely unexpected but enthusiastically received. My cry to God had been to take the anger away, and that prayer appeared to fall on deaf ears for many years. But after the prayer of forgiveness he *did* take it away. It was not easy, and it was not without pain, but it was joyfully rewarding.

God's timing is perfect. His ideas and thoughts are far above anything I could plan. He asked me to forgive when it was the right time. I was not coerced, forced or bludgeoned, but God made it plain that he wanted me to forgive. I had a choice and I made the decision without anyone else even knowing that I was thinking it through. Human insistence could have interfered with the route God had planned; well-meaning people could have told me I had to forgive and scared me off. But God came when he knew I was ready, and then he used that place of forgiveness as a platform upon which to place all the building blocks of my healing.

Forgiveness is required only where there has been a wrong. Perpetrators of abuse use progressive strategies to quieten their conscience. They justify their actions to themselves while acting for their own selfish gratification. But there is no excuse for this sinful behaviour. And forgiving the wrong in no way minimises the serious nature of what has happened.

Over the last few years I have sometimes been asked to talk with women who are depressed, both in individual conversations and in groups. I have been able to do this, having first found God to be my comfort. Knowing the good things God did for me, I can comfort and encourage others. Because of the story of my healing I can say with deep conviction that there is hope, whatever the depth of the pit you may be in.

The love of God I had so longed to feel when I was at the monastery reading Romans 8:38–39 has indeed become my experience:

> . . . neither death nor life, neither angels nor demons, neither
> the present nor the future, nor any powers, neither height
> nor depth, nor anything else in all creation, will be able to
> separate us from the love of God.

My wish is that my experience will bring help to others. I firmly believe that God can use anyone to achieve his purpose, and turn even the worst life experiences into good. Without this belief my history would be one of a complete waste of a life. But I know it is not wasted because, if I can help someone else to pursue their journey to wholeness, it is worth it all.

'He has made everything beautiful, in its time' (Ecclesiastes 3:11).

Notes

Foreword
1. *Total Forgiveness* by R. T. Kendall, London: Hodder & Stoughton, 2003.

Preface
1. 2 Corinthians 1:3b–4.

Chapter Four
1. Woolworths was a general retail store founded in America in 1879 that became a mainstay of the British high street until 2009.

Chapter Five
1. Second verse of the hymn 'Dear Lord and Father of Mankind', words by J. G. Whittier (1872) and tune by F. C. Maker (1887).

Chapter Seven
1. Psalm 18:28.

Chapter Eleven
1. Matthew 6:12, 14–15.

Chapter Twelve
1. The Light House (Christian Care Ministry) Trust provides counselling services in the Midlands area of England.

Chapter Thirteen
1. *Releasing the Scream: Coming to Terms with Childhood Sexual Abuse* by Rebecca Newman, London: Hodder & Stoughton, 1994.

Chapter Fourteen
1. Ellel Ministries is a Christian mission organisation with a vision of welcoming people, teaching them about the kingdom of God and healing those in need.
2. Leviticus 25:8–55.